the only creative process that matters

Finding Ideas and Knowing If They Are Worth Executing From The Smartest Man In The World

saul colt

Staten House

For my Dad.

My biggest fan, biggest cheerleader and the person who taught me to stand out.

He died a few months before I finished this book. A lot of it was written in his final months from his hospital room.

His dying wish was that you would buy multiple copies so I can finally buy a Porsche.

forword by michael nolan

As a former radio guy, entrepreneur, corporate innovator and a retired teenage magician, I never imagined those worlds would collide in the realm of marketing. Yet here I am, writing the foreword for *Saul's Book,* marveling at how a bit of showmanship, a dash of storytelling, and a whole lot of boldness can transform marketing into pure magic. Over the years, I've had the chance to interact with three marketing geniuses.

• **Seth Godin** – who showed me the art of being remarkable (he made me believe a Purple Cow can indeed stop traffic).

• **Mark Ritson** – who schooled me in brand fundamentals and reminded me (with his sharp wit) to never fall for marketing nonsense.

• **Saul Colt** – who proves that the craziest idea in the room, when executed with heart and humor, can turn into marketing gold.

These three marketing gurus all share a common trait: they aren't afraid to break the mold. And trust me, Saul breaks it, sets it on fire, and makes s'mores over the flames – all while teaching you something new.

The Day I Met Saul Colt (Marketing Magic in Action)

I first met Saul at a Word-of-Mouth Marketing convention some years back, and the encounter has since become legend. Saul got in trouble for practicing, well, word of mouth. Instead of buying a boring booth and handing out swag, he wandered the halls with a professional magician to captivate small groups of people, ending each trick with a flourish that magically produced Saul's card.

Being a former professional magician (I hung up my wand at age 14, because once you have done a Magic show in the Olson's living room, there's nowhere left to go.) I was of drawn to the act. Saul and I became fast friends, and we kept up with each other as we both transitioned through a whole bunch of careers, with me ending up teaching adjunct a few Universities while I held down a full-time gig as an Entrepreneur in Residence for a Fortune 10 company.

I *had* to get Saul in front of my MBA students. I invited him as a guest lecturer, and he's been back so often he's practically an honorary professor of mayhem. Students expecting a dry talk on branding suddenly find themselves participating in an impromptu stunt, or having the classroom flipped where they are immersed in a real-life brainstorming session. One minute they're laughing till their sides hurt, and the next they're scribbling down an eye-opening marketing insight wrapped in that shenanigan. It's learning by doing, by laughing, and by experiencing the *wow*.

That's exactly what you're about to get from *Saul's Book*. This isn't your typical marketing tome that puts you to sleep by page 3. Nope. Saul is a master storyteller, and each chapter is a story from the trenches of marketing craziness – from outlandish stunts to ingenious guerrilla campaigns – that **secretly** doubles as an MBA-worthy case study in how to do things differently. You'll giggle at the outrageous lengths he's gone to for a client's attention (did he really hire nude models to walk through a mall? I'll let you discover that yourself), but you'll also come away with actionable lessons in creativity and innovation. Consider each story a magic trick: Saul entertains you with the performance, then reveals the technique so you can repeat it in your own way. The result? You get to laugh *and* learn – the best kind of two-for-one deal.

Buckle Up

So, dear marketer, brand builder, or curious reader, buckle up – you're in for a wild, unconventional ride. Reading this book is a bit like riding shotgun with Saul in a stunt car: exhilarating, a little unpredictable, and ridiculously fun. Along the way, don't be surprised if you find yourself inspired to rethink your next campaign or even hatch a crazy marketing stunt of your own. That tingling sensation? It's your imagination being sparked.

It's rare to find a business book that delivers genuine belly laughs alongside real-world wisdom, but *Saul's Book* is exactly that rare beast. Within these pages, you'll catch glimmers of Seth Godin's iconoclastic spirit and echoes of Mark Ritson's no-nonsense truth-telling. But most of all, you'll hear Saul Colt's one-of-a-kind voice, cheering you on to be brave, be different, and above all, be memorable.

It's my absolute pleasure to introduce you to this adventure. As you turn the page, I'm excited for you – **you're about to learn from one of the most creative marketers on the planet, and have a heck of a good time doing it**. So enjoy the stories, embrace the lessons, and get ready to see marketing through the eyes of a man who truly believes in a little bit of magic.

Welcome to Saul's world. I promise you'll never look at marketing the same way again.

Michael Nolan

(Recovering magician, storytelling educator, and forever fan of marketing done differently)

introduction: the case for being bold

Ever feel like your best ideas are too crazy to share? Good. That means you're on the right track. In a world where consumers are bombarded with thousands of forgettable ads each day, the only way to stand out is to be bold, brave, and maybe a little crazy. Playing it safe is a sure path to invisibility, not something you want when trying to get people talking about your brand. Trust me on this: I've built a career out of doing the kind of marketing stunts that make CEOs nervous and audiences delighted. And guess what? Those brave ideas paid off.

Why go bold? Because word-of-mouth is the most powerful marketing there is. *92% of people trust recommendations from friends and family over any form of advertising, and word-of-mouth generates 2X more sales than paid ads.* You can't buy that kind of trust with a Google ad or a bland billboard. You earn it by giving people something worth talking about. Safe ideas don't inspire conversations; bold ones do. It's that simple.

But bold doesn't mean brainless. There's a method to the madness, and that's what this book is all about. We're going to walk through the whole journey of a world-changing (or at least industry-changing) idea, from the belief that you can pull it off, to dreaming it up, vetting and refining it, selling it to the skeptics in the room, executing it flawlessly, and finally using that success to build a reputation that opens doors for you (and your business) for years to come.

Think of it as a roadmap for turning "Wouldn't it be crazy if…?" into "Can you believe we actually did that?!". Along the way, I'll share war stories from my own escapades: times I gave away thousands of bananas to baffled conference-goers, or threw a rock concert instead of a company Christmas party, or even used a literal cloud to promote cloud software. (Yes, a real cloud. We'll get to that.) These stories are fun, but they're not just here for entertainment, they each carry a lesson you can apply. I want you to steal these ideas, tweak them, and use them yourself.

Most importantly, I want you to feel, by the end of this book, like I'm standing behind you whispering, "Go for it. You've got this. Be as crazy as you need to be." The tone throughout is personal, because this is personal. Creativity takes guts. I know what it's like to have an idea that makes your heart race with equal parts excitement and terror. I also know the regret of not acting on an idea and watching someone else do it later. Consider me your co-conspirator in avoiding that regret.

So if you're ready to stop playing small and start making some creative noise, read on. We'll start with the foundation of it all: the courage to believe in your bold ideas in the first place. By the final chapter, you'll understand how bringing those ideas to life not only wins you customers and fans, but also transforms you into a force to be reckoned with, a personal brand built on brave thinking.

Take a deep breath. Let's dive in. Time to unleash your inner stunt person. Welcome to the ride...and you will notice that by showing you the power of emotional storytelling, creative reframing, and word-of-mouth magic...also, there is some repetitiveness in this book. My friend Stan Lee (ya we were real friends used to say "every comic book should read like it is the first one they picked up". With that in mind, I treated every chapter like a solo experience and explain things and share the same stories a few times but each time I hope I am telling the stories from a different side of the story . The main reason I am doing it is so down the road you can open any chapter at anytime and get a refresher. You should wear this book out and not feel you have to read from the beginning every time .

(#funfact - 95% of the examples in this book are true. If you can figure out the one or two half truths I will buy you a meal.)

1 /
the day i learned to give the world something to talk about

I'M SAUL COLT, founder of the award winning non traditional marketing agency The Idea Integration Co, and I've built a career out of doing the kind of marketing that makes most corporate lawyers break into a sweat. I've been called a lot of things "the smartest man in the world" (long story), a stunt marketer, a professional rebel, but the title I'm proudest of is North America's Best Word of Mouth Marketer. If there's one thing I've learned, it's this: in a world drowning in bland ads and forgettable campaigns, the only marketing that matters is the kind people can't stop talking about. And to get there, you sometimes have to break the rules, ruffle feathers, and occasionally risk looking ridiculous. Trust me, I speak from experience. I've reenacted Evel Knievel's motorcycle jumps to sell accounting software and thrown a rock concert to promote a car-sharing service. I once literally drove across America in an RV just to have breakfast, lunch, and dinner with different customers, day after day, over and over, more than a thousand of them, because I wanted to "make love to the customers" (relax, not literally but there was some necking). What I really mean is I wanted to make them laugh, think, and maybe even cry. More on that in a minute. The point is, I've learned that bold beats boring every time. If you want word of mouth over mindless ad spend, if you want fans instead of just customers, if you want to do marketing that matters, then buckle up you and I are going on a ride.

FROM ZIPCARS TO FLYING MOTORCYCLES: My Strange Path into Creative Marketing

Most marketers start their careers optimistically brainstorming taglines in an office. I started mine by passing out a sledgehammer to take your anger out on the hugh cost of gas and smash a gas guzzling car and then handing out earplugs at a rock concert.

I am bad with years but I was tasked with launching Zipcar in Canada, introducing the car-sharing concept to a market that didn't even know they needed it. Traditional approach? Print some brochures, run some safe ads about convenience. My approach? Host a surprise rock concert with a local indie, surrounded by Zipcar vehicles. We invited our early members and random passersby to come party, because nothing says "use our car-sharing service" like a wall of sound and a chance to win free driving credits? It was unorthodox, irreverent, maybe even a little insane. But you know what? People showed up. They danced, they laughed, they took pictures, and, most importantly, they talked. The next day, the buzz was everywhere: "Did you hear about that Zipcar rock show? What the heck were they thinking?" Exactly. We wanted people to ask what we were thinking, because then we could answer, "reinventing how city folks use cars." By the end of that launch, Zipcar wasn't just a new utility; it was the cool kid in town. We gained thousands of users and a reputation for being fun and bold. I learned an early lesson: be remarkable, literally, worth making a remark about, or be forgotten.

FLASH FORWARD A COUPLE YEARS, and I'm the first marketing guy at FreshBooks, a (then) scrappy online accounting startup. Now, accounting software is about as sexy as wearing socks with sandals. Nobody wakes up dying to chat about invoices and expense reports. So how do you spark word of mouth in a category that cures insomnia? You shock people out of their stupor. Early on, we decided to attend a big tech conference for small business owners. Every other software company was setting up boring booths with pamphlets. We had a loftier ambition: we were going to jump a motorcycle over a pyramid of school buses. Yes, you read that right. We built a ramp, Evel Knievel-style, plastered it with our FreshBooks logo, and had a EK suit made for me to don and pretend to be "The Man." Why? Because it made no damn sense, and that was the point. As crowds gathered (because who wouldn't stop to watch a lunatic on a motor-cycle at a tech conference?), we had our moment to shout what FreshBooks was all about. We turned a dull business conference into a circus, and FreshBooks became the talk of the event.

. . .

THE STUNT RE-CREATED an Evel Knievel jump over school buses to sell accounting software, the kind of crazy idea you only try if you have, well, chutzpah. The payoff was that we purposely ran out of gas before the actual jump and in a self effacing manner I gave everyone who attended a 30 day free trial of FreshBooks for wasting their time and that converted into 500+ new customers. Did some folks think we were nuts? Absolutely. But they remembered us. They told that story to their colleagues later. And FreshBooks went from just another software vendor to the company that almost jumped buses for its customers. Ridiculous? Maybe. Effective? You bet your cape it was.

THAT WASN'T EVEN the wildest thing we did. Shortly after, we took to the road on what I affectionately call the FreshBooks Roadburn Tour. The idea was simple: our software was about saving small business owners time, so we figured we'd spend our time thanking them. We drove coast-to-coast across North America to have meals with as many customers as possible, breakfast in Miami, lunch in Mobile and dinner in I don't remember. Day after day. Sometimes it was ten people at a diner, other times a gathering of fifty at a BBQ joint. Over the course of that journey, we shared three meals a day with over two thousand customers. If I didn't develop scurvy from all the grits, I certainly developed a profound appreciation for the people behind the customer IDs. We laughed over their entrepreneurial war stories, we commiserated about tax season pains, some even teared up recounting how FreshBooks helped them when they were drowning in paperwork. It was marketing in the most human, un-scalable, unforgettable way. When we finally returned home (several pounds heavier from all that pie), something amazing happened: those customers I met became die-hard evangelists. They told their friends about the crazy invoicing company who drove cross-country just to say hello. We didn't just earn users; we earned fans for life. And it reinforced one of my core beliefs: people crave genuine connection and stories worth sharing, not sterile press releases. Sometimes the boldest stunt is simply showing up in person.

These early adventures, the Zipper rock concert, the Evel Knievel jump, the epic road trip, cemented my reputation for what some call "stunt marketing" and what I call having the guts to be interesting. I won't lie, I loved it when Inc. Magazine or Forbes would later name-drop me as a the greatest stunt marketer working today or when Chris Brogan said I'm "exactly who you want representing your company." But the real high wasn't the ego boost; it was seeing the power of creative ideas to create real buzz without a massive ad budget. I learned that a single remarkable idea can generate more attention than a million dollars in bland advertising. And I learned that I wasn't crazy, or at least, if I was, there was a method to the madness. That method, as it turns out, can be distilled, taught, and repeated. It's what this book is about. In the rest of this chapter, I want to share the key principles and frameworks that have guided my approach, my secret sauces, if you will. These are the same filters and processes I've honed over the years to consistently dream up outrageous ideas that work. We're talking about making people Laugh, Think, and Cry, and a little trick from the CIA called WoMBAT that can crack open your creativity like a piñata. So top off your coffee, because now we're getting to the really fun stuff, the part where you learn how to do this too.

THE LAUGH/THINK/CRY Filter: Why Emotion Beats Boring Every Time

Early in my career, I created what I call my "Laugh/Think/Cry" creative filter. It's exactly what it sounds like: any marketing idea I pursue has to make people laugh, think, or cry, preferably all three. That might sound simplistic, but let's unpack it.

LAUGH: Humor is disarming. When you make someone laugh, you get their attention and you lower their defenses. Laughter creates positivity and memorability, there's a reason you probably remember the funniest Super Bowl ad more than the most informative one. In fact, research shows that humor activates both the cognitive and emotional centers of the brain, leading to deeper processing and better memory retention of the message.

IN PLAIN ENGLISH: if you make 'em laugh, they're more likely to listen and remember what you said. Think: After you've got their attention, you need substance. A great campaign should have a smart core that makes people stop and ponder for a second. Maybe it's a twist on conventional wisdom, a clever analogy, or a question that gets them to re-evaluate something.

. . .

THIS IS THE **"THINK"** part, engage the intellect. It's why I often bake a layer of insight or provocation into an idea. For example, our FreshBooks banana stand stunt (we once built a giant banana stand at a conference, a nod to the TV show Arrested Development, with a sign "There's always money in the banana stand", implying there's always money in good business practices). That made people chuckle, sure, but it also made them think about the message behind the joke.

CRY: Lastly, emotion. Now, I'm not literally trying to send people reaching for Kleenex with every marketing campaign (though a tear or two isn't a bad thing). "Cry" is shorthand for touching the heart. Humans remember how you make them feel. If you can stir genuine emotion, inspiration, nostalgia, empathy, even the so-called "happy tears", your message drills itself into their memory. Emotional resonance is powerful; studies have found that purely emotional campaigns outperform rational ones nearly 2-to-1 in effectiveness (one analysis found emotional marketing campaigns had about a 31% success rate, compared to 16% for purely rational campaigns). Why? Because feelings stick. We're wired that way.

SO LAUGH/THINK/CRY became my litmus test. It's the filter I run every idea through: Will this idea make someone laugh out loud? Will it make them pause and think? Could it move them enough to well up, or at least feel a pang of emotion? If the answer is no, then back to the drawing board. But if yes, then I know we have the ingredients of something that can cut through the noise and actually connect with people. When I say in interviews that I "made love to the customers," it's tongue-in-cheek, but it really means I made them Laugh, Think, and Cry, I engaged their full range of emotions. And when you achieve that, you create fans. People might buy a product because it's useful, but they love a product, and tell others about it, because it made them feel something.

LET me give you a quick example of Laugh/Think/Cry in action from my own exploits. Remember that FreshBooks cross-country road trip I took? On the surface, that was a customer-service stunt, a way to show we care. But I designed it very deliberately around this filter. During those customer meetups, I would always do something to get folks laughing first, usually by telling the most embarrassing accounting mistake I ever made or doing some goofy icebreaker. Laughter opened them up. Then I'd ask them to share one tip or lesson from their own business journey , something to get them (and everyone at the table) thinking. And inevitably, someone would share a heartfelt story, maybe about how they almost went bankrupt or how an invoice paid on time changed their life that month, and there'd be this emotional moment, a tear in the eye, a clink of glasses in sympathy. Laugh. Think. Cry. Every dinner, we hit all three notes naturally. The result? Those dinners became legendary in our user community. People posted on blogs about them. One customer told me he hadn't felt that appreciated by any company, ever. And of course, he had to tell all his friends about it. Emotion creates connection, and connection creates word of mouth. It's that simple, and that hard.

NOW, you might be thinking, "That's great, Saul, but how do I consistently come up with ideas that tick those boxes? Do I just sit around waiting for inspiration to strike in the shower?" (Confession: a lot of my best ideas do happen in the bathtub. There's something about bubble baths and creativity, your mileage may vary). But no, you don't have to wait for lightning. There's a process, a technique I've borrowed and adapted from an unlikely source, that can help anyone generate crazy, one-of-a-kind ideas on demand. It's an approach originally used by CIA analysts to think about global threats, and I've co-opted it for marketing (because, hey, running a business sometimes feels like espionage). It's called WoMBAT. And no, it's not the furry Australian marsupial, though those are pretty cool too. WoMBAT stands for "What Might Be All The…". Let's dive into it.

WOMBAT: What Might Be All The… Ways to Unlock Original Ideas

People often ask me, "Saul, how the heck do you come up with this stuff? Do you just have a screw loose?" The truth is, it's not magic or madness (well, maybe a pinch of madness). It's a process, one I honed over years of trial, error, and purposely asking questions differently. And that process is encapsulated in one weird acronym: WoMBAT. The origin of WoMBAT is fascinating: it's used by the CIA to spur creative problem solving in high-stakes situations. Intelligence analysts deal with life-and-death puzzles, and they realized that the way a question is framed can either limit your thinking or blow the problem wide open. There's a cognitive quirk called framing bias, basically, we get fixated on the way a question or task is presented and often miss alternate solutions. WoMBAT is an antidote to that. It literally stands for asking "What Might Be All The…" followed by whatever problem you're trying to crack. By phrasing it that way, you invite your brain to think in possibilities, not answers.

. . .

HERE'S an example the CIA uses internally: If they're trying to locate a target (say a rogue bad guy named Ryan hiding in New York City), the typical person might ask, "Where is Ryan hiding?" That sounds logical, but it's actually a trap, it narrows your focus prematurely. Instead, an analyst will ask, "What might be all the ways to find Ryan in NYC?". That subtle change, what might be all the...forces your mind to generate multiple scenarios and methods. Suddenly you're brainstorming: he might be at his known associate's house, might be using a fake name at a hotel, might be crashing at one of five safehouses, might be disguised as a hot dog vendor in Central Park. Nothing is off the table initially, which is exactly the point. WoMBAT kicks down the door that a narrow question locks.

NOW, how does a marketer use this? Simple. We often fall victim to framing bias in business. We ask questions like, "How do we increase our social media followers?" or "What's the best ad campaign for our new product?" Those are narrow frames, they focus you on one channel or one concept of "best". WoMBAT it instead: "What might be all the ways to get people talking about our product?" or "...all the ways to create an unforgettable launch?" The *"might"* word is key, it suspends judgment. You're not committing to any one idea being the solution, you're just listing possibilities. And "all the ways" blows the doors open for wild, unconventional answers.

WHEN I WAS at FreshBooks and we were looking for ways to get small biz owners to notice us, the normal question would've been: "How can we market our accounting software to small business owners?" Boring! Our first answers would've been equally boring, buy ads in accounting magazines, maybe sponsor a boring webinar. Instead, I literally sat down with my team and said: "What might be all the ways we can get small business owners so intrigued (or shocked) that they have to check us out?" The list we came up with was gloriously nutty. It included things like: hire a marching band to parade through Wall Street handing out our invoices, send carrier pigeons with FreshBooks messages (we actually considered this… PETA, don't @ me), host a free pancake breakfast outside the IRS office on tax day, re-create an Evel Knievel jump over buses (bingo!), get a FreshBooks user to streak at a big industry event with our logo painted on his chest (didn't do that one, sadly). The point is, we went for quantity and creativity first. WoMBAT is about divergent thinking, exploring every corner, before converging on the best idea.

THE WALDO PUZZLE is a great way to illustrate framing bias (I often use this in talks). You know those Where's Waldo? picture books? You're told "Find Waldo" so you pore over the image looking for the striped shirt. You might spend minutes, hours scanning… and in doing so you might completely overlook the hilarious side scenes in the picture (like two random folks rubbing food in their hair in the corner). In one of my articles I quipped: We get so focused on finding Waldo that we miss the hippo dentists!. Businesses do this all the time, fixate on an obvious goal and miss the wild, creative opportunities lurking in the periphery. WoMBAT removes the Waldo blinders. It asks: What might be all the ways to find Waldo? Maybe use a magnet (if he has metal on him), or yell "Free beer at the front!" and see who stands up, or ask why we're even looking for Waldo, maybe he doesn't want to be found! It sounds silly, but this kind of reframing is where innovation lives.

. . .

I ADOPTED WoMBAT as my personal brainstorming framework. Every time I face a marketing challenge or a client asks for "a big idea", I WoMBAT the heck out of it. When I joined Zipcar, the question wasn't "How to get people to sign up for car sharing?" It became "What might be all the ways to make Zipcar the hottest conversation in town?" that led to the rock concert among other ideas. When working with a Canadian sandwich chain later, I asked, "What might be all the ways to get office workers so excited about sandwiches they'd skip work to get one?" (We ended up doing a one-day promo where if you came in a business suit, you got a free sandwich and a handwritten excuse note to give your boss, the press ate it up). This approach ensures you're not just thinking outside the box, you're questioning why the box exists at all. WoMBAT asks: what if there is no box? What if there are dozens of boxes, or what if we could smash the box and build something entirely new from the pieces?

ONE COOL PEDIGREE of WoMBAT is that it's tied to something called the Phoenix Checklist, another CIA method for problem solving. The Phoenix Checklist is basically a list of rigorous questions to interrogate a problem from all angles. It's detailed stuff like "Why is the problem a problem? What isn't the problem? What have you not yet considered?" etc. The spirit of all these techniques is the same: reframe, reframe, reframe until you uncover an approach nobody's tried. In marketing, being first or being weird (or both) is gold. If you do what everyone else is doing, congratulations, you'll get what everyone else is getting (which is tune-out from customers). WoMBAT practically forces originality. It certainly has for me, I owe many of my zaniest, most successful campaigns to a WoMBAT brainstorming session.

· · ·

LET me break down how you can use WoMBAT in your own creative process:

Step 1: Identify the Boring Question. This is the default question everyone else is likely asking. (e.g., "How do we increase market share by 5%?" or "How do I get more attendees to my event?"). Acknowledge that this framing will lead to conventional answers.

Step 2: WoMBAT-ify it. Restate the question starting with "What might be all the..." and include a verb that broadens possibilities. (e.g., "What might be all the ways to turn our product launch into a viral sensation?" or "What might be all the things our ideal customer would share with their friends about this event?"). Notice how the scope widens.

Step 3: List Every Crazy Idea. Now brainstorm freely. Go for at least 10-20 answers. No self-censorship. The ideas should range from practical to patently absurd. In fact, absurd is good at this stage, it means you're stretching. (One of my lists for FreshBooks included "What might be all the ways to make accountants feel like rockstars?" Ideas ranged from "host a Coachella for accountants" to "dress our support team in KISS makeup for a day").

Step 4: Embrace the "Might." Realize you're not committing to any of these... yet. You're just considering them. This mindset prevents the common knee-jerk "that would never work" kill-switch. Leave that for later.

Step 5: Spot the Gems & Polish Them. Among your many ideas, some will jump out as both feasible (with some work) and high-impact. Often, I find the best ideas are the ones that make me a little nervous-excited. You know, that flutter of "Can we actually pull this off? Would they let us do this?" If it's both exciting and scares you a bit, you likely have a winner. Then you refine it, adjust for any real-world constraints, and plan execution.

Step 6: Test Against Laugh/Think/Cry. Now take your favorite idea(s) and run them through the emotional filter. Can we inject humor? Is there a way to add a thoughtful message or a heartwarming touch? This step marries the two frameworks. When WoMBAT gives me a raw concept, Laugh/Think/Cry helps me shape it into a story that will resonate.

BY USING WoMBAT to generate ideas and Laugh/Think/Cry to evaluate and enhance them, you've got a one-two punch for creative marketing that's both original and impactful. It's my not-so-secret formula for coming up with campaigns that get talked about. And remember, getting talked about is the whole point, which brings us to the final part of this chapter: why word-of-mouth beats the pants off traditional advertising, and why being bold is not just fun, but necessary.

SPEAK SOFTLY and Carry a Big Idea: The Power of Word of Mouth over Advertising

Here's a question for you: When was the last time you enjoyed an ad? I mean really enjoyed it, enough to voluntarily tell a friend about it. Maybe a Super Bowl spot or some outrageous billboard, but those are rarer than a unhoused person doing the Macarena. Now, when was the last time you shared a funny story or a cool experience with a friend? Probably within the last 24 hours.

WE HUMANS ARE WIRED to share experiences, not advertisements. That's why I've bet my career on word-of-mouth marketing. It's not just gut feeling telling me that word of mouth is powerful, the data backs it up too.

According to Nielsen (those folks who measure basically everything in media), a whopping 92% of consumers trust recommendations from friends and family more than any form of advertising.

Think about that. You could spend $5 million on a prime-time TV ad, and a single "Hey, you gotta try this, I loved it" from a friend still carries more weight in the mind of your customer. In the U.S., 83% of people say a word-of-mouth recommendation makes them more likely to purchase. Those are not numbers any marketer can ignore. Word of mouth isn't just the most trusted form of marketing; it's arguably the most effective at driving decisions.

SO WHY DON'T companies pour all their effort into generating word of mouth? Well, because it's tricky. It's not as straightforward as buying an ad or sending a coupon mailer.

You can't force people to talk about you, you have to give them something worth talking about. This is why everything I've discussed so far, being bold, emotional, unexpected, is so vital. People don't rave to their friends, "OMG, I got this average product that's exactly like 10 other products." They rave about things that surprise and delight them, things that either solve a problem in an ingenious way or just give them a story to tell. As marketing guru Seth Godin would put it, you need to be a "purple cow" in a field of brown cows, something remarkable and different, or else you're invisible.

BOLD IDEAS GET PEOPLE TALKING. Take Dollar Shave Club, for example. A lot of folks know this story, but it bears repeating because it's basically a word-of-mouth fairy tale. In 2012, this unknown startup spent a reported $4,000 (I think it was more) on a simple, humorous online video ad titled "Our Blades Are Fucking Great." The CEO, Michael Dubin, delivered a deadpan, irreverent monologue that had viewers in stitches and nodding along – it made you laugh (with lines like "I'm good at tennis") and think ("why the heck am I paying so much for razors?"). That video went mega-viral, purely via people sharing it. The result? 12,000 new customers in the first 48 hours. It crashed their website. Within a couple of years, that bold little video propelled Dollar Shave Club to a $1 billion acquisition. They didn't out-spend Gillette on ads; they out-thought them. They won with word of mouth.

OR CONSIDER RED BULL, one of my favorite examples of a brand built almost entirely on stunts and buzz. Red Bull is essentially sugar water with caffeine (a product I have never tried) not exactly a unique product. But from day one,

Red Bull's founder understood he wasn't in the business of selling liquid; he was in the business of selling an idea, the idea that Red Bull gives you wings, adrenaline, excitement. With almost no initial ad budget, Red Bull grew by sponsoring wild events, cliff diving competitions, skateboarding, you name it, and doing insane stunts. They created news instead of buying ads. In 2012, Red Bull pulled off the Stratos space jump, where Felix Baumgartner free-fell from the edge of space 24 miles up. That wasn't an ad; it was literally history in the making, sponsored by Red Bull. Over 200 million people watched some part of that event and saw the Red Bull logo plastered on everything. You can't buy that level of attention easily, it was earned by bold action. An earlier stunt had Felix BASE-jump across the English Channel with a jetpack, which also captured global eyeballs. Red Bull's marketing execs flat-out said these aren't just stunts, they're strategic storytelling: "Instead of expensive, passive traditional advertising, [the founder] became the ultimate buzz marketer". The result? Red Bull today sells billions of cans a year and is the #1 energy drink in the world, all thanks to being the brand everyone talks about when they think of extreme feats and excitement. They've embedded themselves in culture. That's the long-term brand value of bold ideas, they accumulate in the public consciousness. A great stunt isn't one-and-done; if it's truly remarkable, people will recall it years later (and subconsciously, your brand benefits every time they do).

NOW, I'm not saying you need to throw someone out of a balloon in the stratosphere to build your business (though if you have the budget....call me). The principle scales down to any size: focus on creating genuine stories around your brand. Do something unexpected for a customer, stand for a provocative idea, infuse your marketing with humor and heart. Even in B2B or "boring" industries, perhaps especially there, a bold approach can set you light years apart. And here's the kicker: word of mouth isn't just cheaper; it's more sustainable. Ads have a shelf life. That Facebook ad you ran ceases to exist the second your budget runs out. But a word-of-mouth story can live on, get retold, even enter company lore. It's like compounding interest. One great story begets another as you continue to do remarkable things, and pretty soon you have an aura in your market, a reputation that money can't directly buy.

Let's throw in a bit more data because I'm a nerd for this stuff:

One survey found 74% of consumers identify word-of-mouth as a key influencer in their purchasing decisions.

Marketing studies routinely show that referral leads (people who come via recommendation) have higher lifetime value and loyalty than those acquired through other means. It makes sense, if your friend Dave swears by a product, you're not only more likely to try it, you're predisposed to like it because you trust Dave. And guess what? People who come in via word of mouth often continue the chain by telling others, because they themselves were introduced in a memorable way.

KLT = Know/Like/Trust. When you know someone, like someone and Trust someone they have a far bigger influence over you than any ad ever could.

It's a virtuous cycle of free promotion. Meanwhile, trust in traditional advertising keeps dropping; people have ad-blockers, skip buttons, banner blindness. We've all become astonishingly good at tuning out anything that looks or smells like an ad. But a recommendation from a peer? We lean in. That's why I often tell clients: Every dollar you're tempted to spend on ads, consider if you could invest it instead in making an experience so incredible that your customers do the advertising for you. It could be an epic customer appreciation event, or a delightfully bizarre social media challenge, or above-and-beyond service that makes someone's jaw drop. These are not expenses; they're investments in turning your audience into a volunteer marketing army.

LET me give a tangible success story from my own backyard: At FreshBooks, after our series of stunts and that road trip, we noticed something crazy. Without any big increase in ad spend, our user base was growing like wildfire. Why? Because the customers we had were referring others like mad. They'd say, "You gotta try this invoicing thing, they're awesome, they might even send you a cake!" (Yes, I did send out hundreds of cakes once). We tracked referrals with a simple box at sign up asking "how did you hear about us?" and saw a huge uptick in "word of mouth" as a source. It outpaced any other channel. That's when I became an outright evangelist (some would say zealot) for business courage. In fact, I give a talk called "Business Courage" where I basically implore companies to grow a pair (of wings, of course) and take creative risks. Because the downside of a failed stunt is usually a shrug, maybe a little money wasted, or a joke that doesn't land. But the upside of a successful stunt is exponential. It can put you on the map overnight.

. . .

AND EVEN THE "FAILURES" often give you a funny story to tell (which humanizes you, not a bad outcome). I'd argue there's a greater risk in not taking risks. If you play it safe, you blend in, and in today's market, blending in is the fast-track to irrelevance. Or as one of my favorite business mottos goes, **"Safe is risky."**

YOU MIGHT NOT GET FIRED **for playing it safe (short-term), but you sure won't get noticed or promoted either.**

SO CONSIDER this chapter a rallying cry. I want to rally you to be bold. To prioritize word of mouth over billboard impressions, to prefer being talked about over being number one in some fleeting ad ranking. I want you to walk away believing that creativity and daring are not gimmicks, they are your most reliable tools to cut through the noise and earn the only kind of marketing that counts: unpaid, genuine, customer-driven promotion. The rest of this book, I promise, will equip you with the how. We're going to dive deep into finding show-stopping ideas (WoMBAT!), testing and filtering them for maximum emotional impact (Laugh / Think / Cry!), and executing them in ways that make them spread like wild-fire (Word of Mouth!). By the end, you'll not only have a bunch of stories from my journey (including my misadventures, I'll tell you about the time I did get thrown out of a company for pushing it too far, and what I learned), but you'll have a playbook for creating your own legendary campaigns.

IN THE CHAPTERS AHEAD, we'll explore in detail how to systematically generate ideas that break the mold (even if you don't consider yourself "creative"), how to vet those ideas so you don't actually torpedo your brand (there's a fine line between bold and foolish, I'll show you how to walk it), and how to cultivate an audience that amplifies your message for you. But it all starts here, with the mindset we've covered: Marketing that makes people Laugh, Think, Cry, and above all, talk, is marketing that works. Everything else is just noise that people will scroll past.

SO HERE'S my challenge to you as we kick off this journey together: Dare to do something worth talking about. If you're going to spend your precious time and budget on marketing, insist that it checks those boxes. Ask yourself and your team, "Is this idea bold enough? Will anyone care? Does it make me a little excited (or nervous)? Would I tell my friends about this?" And if the answer is no, be brave enough to push for something better. It might be scary, hey, you might get a few raised eyebrows, maybe even an angry board member or two. But as someone who's gone out on many a limb, I can assure you the view from out there is spectacular.

ALRIGHT, that's enough pep talk to open a book. If you're fired up, good, you should be. The fact that you're reading this means you're hungry for a different approach, and I'm absolutely thrilled to share everything I know with you. Great marketing isn't about having the biggest budget or the slickest ads, it's about having the guts to put a truly original idea into the world and let people carry it forward. It's about understanding human emotions and harnessing them in service of your story. It's about laughing, thinking, crying, and sometimes strapping on a helmet and jumping over some buses, to show the world that what you offer is anything but ordinary.

. . .

NOW BUCKLE in and get ready to be bold, be different, and give 'em something to talk about. The world's waiting for your crazy, beautiful ideas, and I can't wait to see you unleash them.

2 /

there are no new ideas (but you can still be original)

I'M GOING to let you in on a little secret: I've never had a completely original idea in my life. Not one. Every brilliant marketing stunt or campaign I've been credited with? It was built from pieces that were already out there, a mash-up of experiences, observations, and random bits of pop culture rattling around in my head. And you know what? That's great news. It means you don't have to conjure genius out of thin air. In fact, the myth of the lone genius struck by a lightning-bolt idea is just that, a myth.

As Mark Twain put it over a century ago, "There is no such thing as a new idea. It is impossible. We simply take a lot of old ideas and put them into a sort of mental kaleidoscope". Twain was right: originality comes from how you combine, twist, and re-imagine what already exists. Your job isn't to invent the next wheel from scratch; it's to notice that the wheel and, say, a motor could make a car. Or that a banana and a stand could make marketing gold.

So take a deep breath and relax. You have all the ingredients you need for creativity, you just have to hunt, gather, and recombine them. Original ideas are found, not created. In this chapter, I'll show you how I find mine. We'll debunk the lightning bolt myth, explore why being a little absurd can unlock big insights, see how constraints improve creativity, and walk through some of my favorite methods (including a weird little career maker called WoMBAT). By the end, I hope you'll hear my voice in your head, cheering you on to find the extraordinary ideas hiding in plain sight in your world. Let's dive in.

ORIGINAL IDEAS ARE FOUND, Not Created (Connecting the Dots)

Creativity is often described as connecting the dots in new ways. Smoothie thrower, Steve Jobs last words were "wow wow wow" (personally I think he was saying ow ow ow" and he also famously said that "creativity is just connecting things." When creative people explain their thought process, he noted, they often feel a bit guilty because it didn't pop out of nowhere, they just saw links that others missed. The brain is a matchmaker, pairing an idea from Column A with one from Column B, and sparking "aha!" moments when an unexpected marriage occurs.

Don't just take it from our friends Steve or Twain, psychology backs this up too. Our brains are association machines, constantly absorbing inputs and looking for novel combinations. Neurologically, idea generation happens when different brain networks interact. There's the logical, focused side (great for solving known problems), and then there's the default mode network, which lights up when you daydream, relax, or take a shower. Ever notice how you get your best ideas in the shower? You're not alone, in one study,

---

72% of people said they have creative insights while showering.

Why? Because a relaxed, undistracted mind wanders freely, bumping into remote connections. The study's lead, cognitive scientist Scott Barry Kaufman, found that a "relaxing, solitary, non-judgmental shower environment" lets the mind roam and sparks creativity. In other words, when you stop trying so hard for a new idea, your brain finds an original twist on an old one.

This is huge: it means that the "lightning bolt" moment isn't a gift from the muses, it's your subconscious connecting dots while you're singing shampoo commercial jingles. The Eureka myth (Newton's apple, Archimedes' bathtub epiphany, etc.) romanticizes the moment of insight and ignores the hours of gathering knowledge and the network of existing ideas that made the insight possible. Original ideas are more excavated than created; they're uncovered by those who are curious and patient enough to dig through the mental sand for that shiny pebble.

So, give yourself permission to steal like an artist (as Austin Kleon says). Hunt for inspiration in strange places. Combine two things that have never been combined before. When I dreamed up one of my more famous stunts, building a banana stand at a tech conference, I wasn't inventing something new. I was blatantly borrowing from the TV show Arrested Development (which had a running joke that "there's always money in the banana stand"). We literally built a replica of the Bluth family's banana stand, and handed out 2,000 actual bananas with our logo on the stickers with a unique url. Totally absurd, absolutely not a "business-as-usual" idea, and it worked like a charm. It drew huge crowds of curious onlookers ("Why the heck is there a nine-foot wooden banana in this boring financial conference?!"), got people talking about us, and drove a ton of traffic to our site via the URL on the banana stickers. The concept of a banana stand wasn't new at all, but applying it in that context was original and effective. We found an idea that was already beloved in pop culture and flipped it into a marketing asset. That's creativity.

Original ideas hide in the space between unrelated concepts. It might be hiding between "accounting software" and "Evel Knievel.". It might be lurking at the intersection of "empty baseball stadium seats" and "customer appreciation event." (Yup, did that too, partnered with the Toronto Blue Jays to fill unused seats with hundreds of our customers, essentially throwing a giant ballpark party on a near-zero budget.) In each case, nothing new was invented, daredevil jumps and baseball games certainly aren't new, but the combination was novel, unexpected, and memorable.

The takeaway: Stop hunting for new ideas, and start looking for new connections. You already have a lifetime's worth of material to work with: your experiences, your favorite stories, your industry's quirks, the weird thing that made you laugh on YouTube last night, all of it is creative fodder. As you begin to see the world as a giant LEGO box of idea bricks, you'll realize you can build infinite castles. And if some structure has been built before? Take it apart and rebuild it differently. That's how originality truly works.

THE LIGHTNING BOLT Myth (and the Slow Burn Reality)

Let's talk about that mythical lightning bolt, the idea that extraordinary ideas arrive in one blinding flash of insight. We idolize the eureka moment. It makes for a great story: "I was just sitting there and BAM, genius struck!" But in my experience (and the experience of basically every creator I know), the lightning bolt is more like a slow burn. The idea may feel sudden when it finally clicks, but it's actually the result of a process, conscious or unconscious, that's been brewing.

Think of your brain as a kitchen. You've been tossing ingredients into the pot for a while: a pinch of that article you read last week, a dash of an old marketing campaign that stuck with you, a tablespoon of frustration from a problem you're facing, and a generous cup of daydreaming. At some point, the mixture simmers into something new, **ding!**, the idea is ready. It tastes like nothing you've cooked before, but every ingredient was already in your pantry. The lightning bolt myth tricks us into waiting passively for inspiration to strike. The reality is you can actively stir the pot to encourage those ingredients to combine in interesting ways.

Here's how I stir the pot when I need ideas: I deliberately expose myself to absurdity and humor (to loosen up my thinking), I add constraints (weirdly enough, constraints often increase creativity), and I use a framework of asking bigger questions (that WoMBAT thing I teased). We'll get into each of those in detail. But the common thread is that none of these methods rely on divine intervention. They're repeatable techniques that provoke your imagination and tease out the insights already percolating in your mind.

I also make sure to give myself space for incubation. That

can mean taking a walk, taking a shower, or yes, in my case, taking a bath. (True confession: I do some of my best thinking naked, submerged in bubbles. I've joked on stage that I do my own stunts and my own nudity, and it's kind of true! The bathtub is my safe space for crazy idea generation and I want to add one in our boardroom.) Science backs this up: as we saw, a relaxed mind is an inventive mind. So if you've been grinding on a problem for hours with no breakthrough, do yourself a favor: step away and do something completely different. Let your default mode network take over, let your mind wander. The idea will come, often when you least expect it.

The point is, don't buy the myth that some people are just lightning rods for ideas and you're not. If you haven't been zapped by genius out of the blue, you're not broken, you're normal. The "lightning bolt" moments will come when you've gathered plenty of sparks and given them a chance to ignite. And you can accelerate that process. Here's how.

EMBRACE Absurdity and Humor (Laugh Your Way to Ideas)

If you walk into our office at The Idea Integration Co. during a brainstorm, you might think we've lost our minds. We're tossing out the most ridiculous, off-the-wall concepts you can imagine. A lot of laughter, some terrible puns, impressions, maybe jumping on couches like a young Tom Cruise, it can feel more like a comedy writers' room than a marketing meeting. That's 100% intentional. Humor is our secret weapon for idea generation. Being a little silly (okay, a lot silly) is not just fun, it's productive. Research has shown that humor boosts creative thinking. One Psychology Today article summarized that humor "advances and promotes divergent thinking", and it cited a study finding a high correlation between a person's sense of humor and their creativity.

For context, that's a much stronger link than the correlation between creativity and IQ.

> Best ideas come as jokes. Make your thinking as funny as possible.

In plain terms: being able to laugh at Pee Wee Herman or Conan O'Brian come up with a goofy pun might indicate a more creative mind than acing an intelligence test.

Why does absurdity help? Because creativity thrives when the stakes feel low and the possibilities feel vast. Humor signals your brain that you're in a safe, playful mode. It lowers inhibitions and quiets the inner critic that's constantly saying "That's too dumb" or "That will never work." When you laugh, you loosen up. In that loosened-up state, you're willing to explore odd associations and wild what-ifs. Jokes often involve connecting unrelated concepts (surprise, just like creative ideas). As one author put it, humor increases our "cognitive flexibility", our ability to think in unconventional ways.

I've found that an absurd suggestion can be the key to unlocking a great idea. In brainstorms I'll often challenge my team (or myself) to come up with the most outrageous, stupid, wrong idea first. Why? Because once the worst idea is out there, nothing else looks scary. It's like stretching before a workout. If we start by jokingly pitching "Let's send our next product launch into space on a rocket piloted by a chimpanzee," then suddenly a more grounded creative idea doesn't seem so unattainable (or risky) by comparison. The absurd sets the outer limit of possible, and everything inside that limit feels more reachable. Plus, sometimes within that joke idea, there's a germ of brilliance. (Hmm, space...chimpanzee...maybe we really could do a space tie-in, minus the primate pilot, what about a zero-gravity product demo video?). Absurdity breeds originality by breaking patterns.

There are practical techniques to leverage this. One is borrowed from improv comedy: the "Yes, and..." rule. In improv, no matter what crazy scenario your partner presents, you're trained to respond with "Yes, and...", accepting their idea and building on it. You never kill the momentum by saying "No, that wouldn't happen." In creative brainstorming, adopting a "yes, and" mindset is game-changing. It means when someone throws out a wacky idea, you look for the merit or the interesting kernel in it and expand, rather than shooting it down. For example, if a colleague says, "Maybe our accounting software needs a mascot... like a giant dancing calculator," the knee-jerk managerial response might be "That's off-brand, moving on." A "yes, and" response might be, "Yes, and what if that calculator mascot crashed an actual accounting conference dance floor, Flashmob style?" Now we're cooking! That second idea might evolve into something usable, maybe an attention-grabbing conference stunt, whereas a dismissal would have left us with nothing. Yes, and keeps the creative doors open.

Another technique: brainwriting instead of (or before) brainstorming. Traditional brainstorming, with everyone shouting ideas, often favors the loudest voices and the first ideas mentioned. It turns out, it's not the best way to get original ideas from a group. Research has found that group brainstorming is less effective than we assume, people unconsciously start conforming to whatever ideas pop up first. By contrast, "brainwriting" (where individuals write down ideas on their own, then share) leads to more ideas and more original ideas.

In fact, in Professor Leigh Thompson's studies at Kellogg School of Management, teams using brainwriting generated 20% more ideas than traditional brainstormers, and their ideas were 42% more original on average.

Even more striking, no face-to-face brainstorming group has been shown to outperform a brainwriting group in published research. That's a big deal! It means if you simply have people ideate independently (on paper or digital notes) for even 5-10 minutes before group discussion, you'll get a richer pool of raw material. In my sessions, I'll often say, "Alright, everybody take five minutes in silence to jot down as many ideas as you can, no matter how crazy." Only after that do we go around and share. It levels the playing field and brings out the quieter folks' brilliance (often introverts have some of the wildest ideas, but they won't fight a loudmouth for talking space). So try brainwriting with your team, it's a simple hack that yields great results.

One more tool in the absurdity toolbelt: Mash-up creativity. This is one of my personal favorites. When I feel stuck, I force a mash-up: I'll randomly pick two unrelated things and ask, "What would a combination of these look like?" We touched on this earlier, it's essentially connecting dots that don't obviously go together. Some legendary products and ideas came from mash-ups. A sports shoe + a fashion logo = Air Jordan (basketball + street fashion culture). A phone + a computer = the smartphone. In marketing stunts, I love mash-ups because they naturally produce the unexpected. When FreshBooks was young and we needed attention, I looked at what our target audience (small business owners) liked and what they never expected from accounting software. They liked baseball, they did not expect us to throw a baseball extravaganza. Mash-up time: we partnered with the Blue Jays to host hundreds of clients at a game, turning an empty upper deck into a FreshBooks fan section. We mashed accounting with sports fandom, and it got people talking (and probably made a few more Jays fans in the process). Think about what you can mash up in your world: Your industry + a trending meme?

Two products that have never been offered together? An old-school nostalgic experience + modern tech? Make a habit of saying "What if X met Y?" The results will often be amusing, and occasionally, amazing.

The underlying principle here is freedom to play. Give yourself and your team permission to be goofy. In our office, no idea is too stupid to voice (I mean, I once hired a Whitney Houston impersonator to preform at a party the day after Whitney Houston passed away. We didn't say anything to anyone and just announced during the night "Ladies and gentleman, please welcome Whitney Houston"). When you embrace absurdity, you're really embracing possibility. You're saying, "All ideas are welcome here, even the wild and weird." It creates a culture where creativity can thrive without fear. And guess what? Absurdity and humor not only lead to better ideas, they make the creative process fun. You want your team looking forward to idea meetings, not dreading them. Joy is an underrated business tool. So go ahead, crack a joke, be a little irreverent. Creativity is serious business, but it flourishes in a playful environment.

PUT Constraints to Work (Why Limits Spark Creativity)

Now it's time to get paradoxical: After telling you to embrace freedom and play, I'm going to tell you to embrace constraints and limitations. Sounds like a buzzkill, right? Shouldn't true creativity be about boundless "blue sky" thinking? Surprise, research and real-world experience say constraints can be a catalyst for creativity. In fact, many creatives will tell you that a blank page or unlimited options isn't liberating; it's paralyzing. (Ever sat in front of an empty Word doc and felt your mind empty out in response? Yeah, me too.) On the other hand, when you have some boundaries, even arbitrary ones, your brain kicks into gear to solve the puzzle. Necessity is the mother of invention, as the proverb goes, and necessity is just a fancy word for constraint.

There's plenty of evidence that creativity loves constraints. One review of 145 studies on innovation found that teams were actually more innovative when they embraced constraints rather than trying to remove them. Margaret Boden, a renowned cognitive scientist who studies creativity, said it well: "Constraints, far from being opposed to creativity, make creativity possible.". Think of a sonnet: the rigid 14-line rhyme scheme has inspired poets for centuries to come up with ingenious wordplay and metaphors within that tight box. Or consider how Twitter's old 140-character limit (a severe constraint) sparked a whole new form of wit and concise expression online. When you have limited resources, time, or options, you're forced to recombine and reimagine what you do have in more inventive ways.

I've lived this truth over and over in my career. Early on at FreshBooks, we didn't have a fat marketing budget. Constraint. So we got creative by necessity, hence antics like the banana stand. That stunt was successful partly because we were constrained to a small booth space and a shoestring budget. We couldn't out-spend the big sponsors on glitzy displays, so we had to out-think them. A big limitation we turned into an advantage was our sense of humor and will-ingness to be different. That didn't cost a thing. The banana stand was literally wood, paint, bananas, and chutzpah. The result: a buzz that thousands of dollars in banner ads wouldn't have achieved. Or look at that Blue Jays event: instead of seeing an empty stadium section as a downer, we saw it as an asset (empty seats = available real estate for our narrative). We begged the Jays to let us fill it, and because their constraint was poor attendance, they agreed cheaply and we bought a lot of beer and hot dogs. Win-win.

Sometimes I even create artificial constraints as a creativity exercise. I might say, "Okay, what if we only had $100 to launch this campaign? Go." Suddenly, all the pricey, default ideas fall away and scrappier, more inventive ideas emerge (like trading resources with partners, DIY solutions, leveraging free media, all those fun "growth hack" type ideas). Or I'll impose a format constraint: "What if we could only convey this message in a single Tweet?" or "How would we pitch this using only emojis?" Silly? Yes. But it forces a fresh approach. It's like restricting a painter's palette to three colours; they'll often surprise you with new techniques to compensate.

Constraints also help because they give you a clear box to think outside of.

I love how one innovator, Tess Callahan, phrased it: "What if the key to thinking outside the box is to create a box to think outside of?".

Exactly. Define the parameters (the box) and then your mission becomes how to stretch and bend within and just beyond those walls. No box at all, and you're just floating in every direction, that's hard.

Let me give you a dramatic example: a few years back, I worked with a client who insisted on a crazy constraint, they wanted a huge PR stunt but absolutely no paid media and no traditional ads. At first this seemed like a handcuff. But that constraint pushed us into what I call "stunt marketing" mode completely, we had to make something so inherently shareable and newsworthy that it would spread on its own. We ended up staging a food product sampling inside the commuter trains coming into the business core from the far away suburbs. It cost peanuts compared to a national ad buy, and it generated half a million impressions and a ton of user-generated buzz and I am sure a lot of people walked into their office and bragged that they were on the cool train. Would we have proposed something that outrageous if the client had just said "eh, here's a million bucks, buy some TV spots"? Maybe not. Constraint = creativity unlocked.

The key with constraints is to embrace them as creative challenges rather than annoying limitations. Flip your mindset to "Because I only have X, I get to be creative" instead of "I only have X, I can't do anything." It's like MacGyver with a piece of gum and a paperclip figuring out how to escape the trap, half the fun is the limitation. And when you do come up with the solution, it often has an elegance and originality born directly from the constraint.

If your constraints feel too suffocating, one trick is to add a playful or arbitrary constraint on top, to spark ideas. For example, if you're a marketer tasked with a by-the-numbers product launch (boring constraint), challenge yourself with an additional constraint: "Alright, how would I launch this product if I could only use 1950s technology?" or "How would I do it if I had to make the CEO's pet the hero of the campaign?" It sounds dumb, but these exercises force you to think laterally about the problem. You can, of course, drop the silly constraint later, but you might retrieve a quirky idea in the process. It's all about seeing your situation from new angles.

Book store owner, Jeff Bezos once said, "Frugality drives innovation, just like other constraints do. One of the best ways to get out of a tight box is to invent your way out.". He grew Amazon with that mentality, many early Amazon innovations were born from constrained resources. So, the next time you're cursing a tight budget or a tight deadline or a lack of staff, remember: this is your moment to shine. Constraints separate the true creatives from the pretenders. They force you to find the original path that nobody saw because it was easier to throw money or resources at the problem. Embrace the challenge and get excited, you're about to find a truly original solution.

IN THE NEXT CHAPTER (#3, yo), we'll get our hands dirty with the WoMBAT method, step by step, so you can start finding your own "hippo dentists" hiding beyond the Waldos of your industry. After that, we'll refine those ideas with Laugh/Think/Cry so you know which ones will really hit people in the gut (in the best way). And finally, we'll delve into the mechanics of making ideas spread and how to build campaigns that practically market themselves through buzz.

THIS ISN'T JUST THEORY, it's worked for me, and it will work for you. So let's do this. Because life's too short for boring marketing. And if we do this right, if you laugh, think, and maybe cry a little along the way, then by the final page of this book you'll be ready to create the kind of marketing that fills your business with raving fans. As Jimmy V said, "That's a full day. That's a heck of a day." Let's make every day of your marketing journey a heck of a day.

3 /
ask "what might be all the...?" (the wombat framework)

ALRIGHT, time to go deep on my not-so-secret weapon: WoMBAT. (this is what I meant in chapter one about being repetitive but like I said there I am re-explaining so you can pick up any chapter years from now and just dive in without a full re-read). WoMBAT is an acronym: "What Might Be All The...". It's a framework and mindset I've adopted (originally inspired by a technique reportedly used in the CIA for problem solving) that basically forces you to reframe your question and think expansively. Whenever I'm faced with a challenge or need a big idea, I WoMBAT it.

HERE'S HOW IT WORKS. Normally, when trying to solve a problem, we ask a pretty narrow question, often without realizing it. For example, a typical marketing brief might lead you to ask, "How do we promote this new product launch?" That seems fine at first glance. But it's actually limiting, it presupposes the way we're going to do it (promotion) and maybe even the channels. WoMBAT would have you tweak that to, "What might be all the ways we could make people fall in love with this product?" Do you feel how much broader and juicier that question is?

Instead of looking for one answer, WoMBAT is about listing all the possible avenues, including the weird, the impractical, the "out there." It's brainstorming the question itself. The CIA uses this to war-game scenarios: they don't ask "Will X happen, yes or no?", they ask "What might be all the ways X could happen?". By doing that, they uncover scenarios that a narrow question would miss.

IN A BUSINESS CONTEXT, WoMBAT is your antidote to framing bias, which is a fancy term for getting tunnel vision on the obvious problem and missing the hippo dentists in the corner. (Quick sidebar: Remember when I said framing bias is like doing a "Where's Waldo?" puzzle, you get so fixated on finding Waldo in his striped shirt that you overlook the absurd but interesting scene in the background, like two people flashing their sexy bits. In business, that means we might focus on the same old solutions and miss a wild opportunity lurking off to the side.

FROM SAFE QUESTIONS to Bold Ideas

Most people brainstorm by looking for the answer. WoMBAT flips that. It asks what all the answers might be, especially the outrageous ones. By framing a challenge as "What might be all the... (X)", you give yourself permission to consider everything. No idea is too out-there at first. This matters because the obvious ideas (the block parties, the boring press releases) don't get you noticed. The unexpected ones do. And you only find those by digging beyond the first answers.

THERE'S SCIENCE BEHIND THIS, by the way. Researchers at MIT found that in 80% of cases, switching to a "question burst" brainstorming (i.e. coming up with nothing but questions) reframes the problem and yields at least one valuable new idea. Not only do people generate more ideas than when they just blurt out solutions, but they also feel more excited and positive about the challenge. Even at Microsoft, they discovered that when teams brainstorm with open questions, more people contribute and nobody feels the pressure to already have "the brilliant answer". In other words, asking "What might be all the…?" turns brainstorming from a test of smarts into a playground for imagination. And that's where the magic happens.

Let me show you how WoMBAT works in the real world, with a few of my favorite (and yes, slightly insane) examples from my own career.

WOMBAT IN ACTION: The Harlem Party That Never Was

One of my all-time favorite ideas was a pitch we developed for a major TV network. They had a new show set in 1970s Harlem, think underground clubs, crime bosses, soul music, and afros. The network wanted a big launch event to get attention. Their early brainstorms? Painfully safe. They suggested the usual: maybe a block party or private event, invite the actors, play some music, serve a themed cocktail. You know, the kind of vanilla event everyone's done a million times. "It'll be fun," they said. Sure, but nice enough isn't memorable. No one was going to care or even remember it by the next morning.

So we stepped in and, you guessed it, went full WoMBAT on it. We asked ourselves:

What might be all the ways to bring 1970s Harlem to life for people today?

What might be all the ways to show not just the setting, but the soul of this show?

What might be all the untapped, gritty details of that era that could surprise and delight an audience?

THESE QUESTIONS BLEW the brief wide open. Suddenly a generic party wasn't even in the top 50 ideas. If we wanted to capture the swagger, rhythm, and danger of '70s Harlem, we had to do more than serve drinks and play retro music. We had to transport people.

Instead of jumping straight into decor and venue discussions, we dove into Harlem's culture. (No Pinterest mood boards here, culture first, slides later.) Our team binge-watched Blaxploitation films like Super Fly and Shaft, read books on Harlem's history, stared at pictures of Pam Grier (she and Linda Carter were my first crushes) soaked up oral histories and museum archives. We even studied the local criminal underworld, and one thing practically leapt off the page: the Harlem "numbers racket." This was an underground lottery that thrived in the community back in the day. It was illegal, gritty, a little dangerous, but also hopeful, people played with dreams of hitting it big. In a weird way, the numbers game captured the spirit of Harlem in that era: hustle, hope, crime, survival all mixed together.

And we thought, what might be all the ways to build an event around that?

The Big Idea: Play the Numbers, Win the Night

Our WoMBAT-fueled answer: Bring back the Harlem numbers game, and let people experience the two sides of that world. We pitched a multi-layered, immersive stunt: on the streets of Harlem and NYC, we'd run fake "number parlors" staffed by actors in 70s wardrobe, letting people play the old lottery. But instead of cash, the winners would get golden tickets to one of two extreme Harlem experiences:

Prize 1: The Velvet Rope Nightclub. We'd host an exclusive 1970s-style club night. Think a Studio 54 vibe in uptown Manhattan: velvet ropes, bouncers, era-appropriate cocktails, Curtis Mayfield and Aretha Franklin on the turntables, and the stars of the show mingling with guests on the dance floor. A full-on disco inferno fantasy come to life.

PRIZE 2: The 1977 Blackout Loot. This one was wild. We'd recreate the infamous 1977 blackout on a controlled city block. Streetlights out, everything dark except a boom box blaring music from a car hood. Our "lottery winners" would get to partake in (legal) looting, we'd set up storefronts dressed to look like '77 electronics and record shops, then fill them with show-themed swag: faux vintage stereos, vinyl records, funky 70s fashion pieces, you name it. When the lights went out, winners could raid the stores and grab everything. They'd walk away with bags of cool loot and, more importantly, a hell of a story. For a few hours, they would feel the chaos, thrill, and edgy fun of that era's Harlem.

WE BASICALLY WANTED to bottle the feeling of the show and pour it on our guests. It was outrageous, sure, but it hit every note the network said they wanted. It was rooted in real Harlem history and culture. It was experiential and participatory. It had media buzz potential out the wazoo (naked city block blackout, anyone?). And it would make people feel something, excitement, nostalgia, adrenaline, rather than just "oh neat, free drinks".

SO WHAT HAPPENED? They passed. In the end, the network's execs got cold feet. They retreated to the familiar and approved a standard party with a signature cocktail (whenever I hear signature cocktail my eyes roll way back into my brain). I remember seeing a blurry photo from that event pop up on Instagram... a handful of likes, zero press, zero cultural impact. Meanwhile, our big bold idea never saw the light of day (or the dark of night, as it were).

IT WAS A BUMMER, no doubt. But I consider that Harlem concept one of the best ideas I've ever had that never got made. And it taught me,, and hopefully the client, a valuable lesson: Safe ideas feel safe. Brave ideas change culture. The block party felt safe, and it produced exactly zero memorable moments. Our WoMBAT-inspired idea, on the other hand, scared them a bit, which is exactly why it had the potential to break through. That's the difference between marketing for impressions and marketing for impact. If you want the latter, you have to be willing to push boundaries.

. . .

(SIDE NOTE: We don't always lose pitches. A lot of clients do buy into the crazy stuff, and they're the ones who make history. But I wanted to share this story because not every bold idea sells, especially if a company's courage hasn't caught up to its ambitions. Creative bravery is a muscle, sometimes the client needs to flex it a bit more.)

WOMBAT IN ACTION: The Naked Truth About a Belt Campaign

Speaking of brave ideas, let's talk about belts. Yes, belts, those leather things holding up your pants. Not exactly the sexiest product, right? A few years back I had a tv production deal to make a pilot around this very process. Every week we were going to feature a deserving brand and show the ideation process and pull off a crazy stunt. For the pilot we wanted to work with one of our favourite people and brands, a cool indie leather company called Jon Wye (they make graphic leather belts by hand).

Now, belts are basically the forgotten fashion accessory. Think about it, shirts, shoes, jackets get all the love. Belts? An afterthought. So the question we started with was, "What might be all the ways to make people actually notice a belt?"

Well, here's one: make the belt the only thing they're wearing.

SO WE COOKED up a little guerrilla experiment. On a busy afternoon, we rolled into one of the biggest shopping malls in Canada, right at the peak of the lunch rush. The food court was packed, hundreds of people slurping noodles and chowing burgers. And then... we put on a fashion show. A very, uh, minimalist fashion show. We sent out one male and one female model, completely naked, except for, you guessed it, their Jon Wye belts. Nothing but belts and birthday suits, strutting right through the food court like it was Paris Fashion Week.

NOW, we hadn't exactly asked the mall's permission (rebellious streak, remember?). This was a full-on stunt. We had camera crews with GoPros stationed to capture every angle, and we had exit routes planned in case security booted us in the first 10 seconds. In fact, we had the whole thing timed in our heads: If we get 15 seconds of footage, that might be enough; 30 seconds would be amazing; anything more than that is gravy.

WHAT HAPPENED WAS beyond our wildest expectations. The crowd gasped, then started cheering and laughing. And the mall cops? They were so utterly stunned by the sight of two naked models in broad daylight that they froze. I kid you not, these two security guards just stood there, mouths open, probably thinking "Is this actually happening?!" We blew right past our 10-second ejection plan... 30 seconds... a minute... they still hadn't stopped the show! Our models did a nice slow catwalk circuit, waving and showing off their one article of clothing (the belts). Two minutes went by and security still hadn't recovered. We hadn't planned for that! Eventually, after about three minutes, an eternity in stunt time, we wrapped it up ourselves. The models casually walked out, we grabbed our cameras and slipped away before the mall cops even remembered how to speak.

THE RESULT: an amazing piece of viral content for the client and a story no one in that food court will ever forget. The video spread online, and Jon Wye became "that cool belt brand with the naked runway show." Mission accomplished. And not a single person who saw that stunt will ever look at a belt the same way again.

NOW, would every brand agree to this lunacy? Heck no. This was full of balls and vagina (literally and figuratively). But it illustrates something important about using WoMBAT: when you allow yourself to ask "What might be all the ways to make a belt unforgettable?" you might land on an idea that scares you at first. And that's okay. In fact, that's good.

CREATIVE MARKETING LIVES on that line between exciting and uncomfortable. I often tell clients,

---

"My job isn't to drag you all the way into Crazytown; it's to find where your comfort zone ends and push you just a couple steps beyond".

With Jon Wye, those couple steps beyond happened to involve public nudity because his brand is awesome and so is he, but hey, it worked for them. And once you take a leap and see that the world doesn't explode, you can take a slightly bigger leap next time. That's how a brand builds creative courage. Today the internet is noisier than ever, if you only do what everyone expects, you'll get lost in the shuffle. Sometimes you've got to run naked through the food court (metaphorically... or not) to get people's attention. As I like to say, if you're only going up to the line of "normal," you're gonna get overlooked in a heartbeat.

WOMBAT IN ACTION: Turning Farmers into Superheroes

Not every WoMBAT idea has to involve crime bosses or naked models. Sometimes it's about taking a mundane marketing task and flipping it on its head. One client of ours, sells high-tech tools and services for farmers, things like digital crop monitoring, analytics, etc. Important stuff, but not exactly thrilling to the average person. They wanted to showcase their product lineup in a catalog or brochure. Yawn, right? Typically you'd make a nice glossy pamphlet with product shots and call it a day. But we asked, "What might be all the ways to make a product catalog not boring as dirt?" More specifically, "What might be all the ways to make farmers feel like absolute superheroes using these products?"

The answer we landed on: turn the catalog into a comic book.

WE LITERALLY CREATED a comic book where the heroes are farmers saving the world, armed with the tools and tech of our client in their arsenal. Picture a stoic farmer cape blowing in the wind, using satellite data to fight off a pest invasion like it's a supervillain, or deploying climate analytics to save a town from drought, all drawn in bold, colorful comic panels. Every page of this "catalog" told a story of how modern farming tech is basically a superpower. And of course, in each story the product line was the trusty gadgetry enabling our heroes' feats.

Why a comic? Because it's fun. It flips the script. Farmers (and the agriculture industry folks) aren't used to seeing themselves portrayed like the Justice League. By presenting the product info in a graphic novel format, we not only made it more engaging to read, we made the audience feel awesome. We took the everyday heroism of farming, and trust me, farmers are heroes, feeding the planet and all, and gave it a bit of mythic shine. And you can bet that comic-book catalog didn't get tossed in a drawer like another forgettable brochure. It was shared around, talked about, and helped our client stand out as an innovative, story-driven brand.

· · ·

THIS IS another hallmark of WoMBAT thinking: re-imagining the expected format. A boring catalog becomes a thrilling comic book. A product demo becomes a viral stunt. A launch party becomes an immersive time-travel experience. When you routinely ask "What might be all the different ways we could do this?", you eventually hit on one that makes you go "Wait... can we do that?", and that's when you know you're onto something great.

(I WROTE the first draft of it before handing it off to a professional comedy writer, one of the brilliant folks we have on our team from Mad Magazine and The Simpsons, to punch it up. The final result was a hundred times funnier and more clever than what I started with. It was a true collaboration of geeky marketing and comic book nerdery. Proud moment for me, honestly.)

THE WOMBAT MINDSET: Embrace the "What If...?"

By now you can probably tell, I'm obsessed with this approach. WoMBAT isn't just a brainstorming trick, it's a creative mindset. It's about constantly challenging the framing of a problem. Too often in business we ask questions that are really just veiled instructions: "How do we do XYZ campaign?" implicitly says "We've decided on a normal campaign, just execute it." WoMBAT blows that up. It asks bigger, sometimes uncomfortable questions: "What might be all the ways to achieve the real goal here?" Maybe the real goal isn't a campaign at all, but a PR stunt, or a community movement, or something totally unexpected.

If you've read the earlier chapters on the creative process, you know we've talked about things like breaking out of mental ruts, thinking sideways, being fearless. Consider

WoMBAT the tool that ties all that together. It's the question that forces you to be fearless and think sideways. It has certainly made me braver and more imaginative over the years. Every time I use it, I'm essentially daring myself: don't wuss out, give me the crazy version too.

And let me tell you, the crazy version is almost always where the gold is. Maybe you dial it back 10% for practical reasons, maybe you have to convince a boss or client and take baby steps, but that bold idea is going to shine far brighter than the safe one. As the saying goes, "If your ideas don't scare you a little, they're probably not big enough."

WoMBAT is about making it safe to voice the "scary" ideas by getting them all on the table. It's much easier to rein in a wild idea than to pep up a boring one. Or as I like to put it, I'd rather calm down a wild stallion than try to ride a dead horse. WoMBAT ensures there are a few wild stallions in the barn.

WOMBAT WORKS IN ANY SCENARIO. If you're launching a startup, don't ask "How do I market my startup with no money?" Ask, "What might be all the things I could do to get people super excited about our mission?" Your list might include wild stuff like staging a protest, creating a secret society, hosting a free concert, writing an open letter on a billboard, partnering with a rival, tattooing the logo on my forehead... whatever. The point is not that you'll do all those things; it's that by listing them, you might stumble on a gem or two you can do. It widens your solution space.

THE WOMBAT MINDSET also encourages you to ask better questions as a habit. Often, when we feel stuck, it's because we're asking the wrong question. For instance, instead of "How can we win more customers?" you might ask, "What might be all the reasons potential customers hesitate to sign up, and how could we flip each hesitation into a wow moment?" Notice how that second question is already pointing to creative answers (maybe your sign-up process is boring, so turn it into a game; maybe people are unsure of value, so find an outrageous way to demonstrate value upfront, etc.).

I LITERALLY KEEP a sticky note on my monitor that says "What might be all the…" to remind me to go wide. It's a license to ideate with abandon. And yes, often the first ideas on that list will be obvious ones (get those out), then they'll get progressively stranger, and that's where the magic is. Usually idea number 29 on the list is way cooler than idea number 3. It takes patience to WoMBAT, you're essentially forcing yourself past the first acceptable answers into the territory of "hmm, what else, what else?" But trust me, that's where the original ideas live.

IF YOU WORK WITH A TEAM, make WoMBAT a part of your culture. When someone comes with a proposal, ask them, "Great, but what might be all the other ways to tackle this?" Create a running list on a whiteboard. You'll be amazed at how this practice surfaces ideas that never would've emerged otherwise. It also helps you compare radically different approaches, maybe the best solution is a combination of two ideas from that list.

ONE MORE THING: WoMBAT isn't just about quantity; it's about perspective shifting. It nudges you to consider every angle. In the Waldo puzzle example, the WoMBAT approach was, "What might be all the ways to find Waldo?" Someone joked "hire Sherlock Holmes" or "use AI" or "flip the puzzle upside down". Those aren't literal plans, but they indicate a mindset of approaching the problem from the side door instead of head-on. That's often what originality is, sidestepping conventional thinking. As a marketer, if everyone else is asking "How do we make a better banner ad?", I want to be the one asking "What might be all the ways to make advertising obsolete for this launch?" That question might lead me to focus on product-led growth or community building instead of ads, a whole new playbook that stands out.

TO SUM UP WOMBAT: It's about expanding your field of view. Don't stare yourself blind at the same target everyone else is aiming for. Soften your gaze and see the periphery, the hippo dentists, the hidden bananas (we'll get to those next). The world is full of offbeat, brilliant solutions waiting for someone to ask the right open-ended question. Be that someone. WoMBAT the heck out of your challenges and you'll find your original idea.

THERE'S ALWAYS Money in the Banana Stand (Noticing Hidden Assets)

You've probably gathered by now that I have a soft spot for the banana stand story. It is a tale that I'll be telling that tale until I'm 90 and honestly the way I feel I may be 90 already. I love the story because it is just such a perfect example of turning something ordinary (bananas) into marketing gold through creativity. But there's a broader lesson here beyond "be funny with bananas." The lesson is: Notice the assets and opportunities that everyone else overlooks.

. . .

ON THE TV show Arrested Development, the catchphrase "There's always money in the banana stand" was literal, the characters had hidden cash in the walls of their banana stand. In real life marketing, "money in the banana stand" is a metaphor for untapped resources or angles sitting right under your nose.

WE TOUCHED on this with the Blue Jays example: those empty stadium seats were a leftover asset. The team wasn't using them, so they had potential value to us. Every business, every brand, every individual has "banana stands", assets that aren't being used to their full potential. It could be physical space, digital space, existing content, byproducts, partnerships, customer goodwill, you name it. Creativity often means spotting that undervalued asset and doubling down on it in a clever way.

FOR FRESHBOOKS in the early days, our banana stand at that conference was an underused asset in two forms: one, our sense of humor and cultural savvy (which most competitors in the financial software space definitely did not leverage), and two, actual bananas (seriously, who thinks of bananas as a marketing medium?). Instead of giving out boring branded stress balls or pens like every other booth, we gave out something people actually wanted and found amusing, free fruit with a joke attached. Bananas were cheap, healthy, and on-theme with our inside joke.

THAT'S A HIDDEN ASSET: the ability to take a cheap commodity and imbue it with a story.

· · ·

ASK YOURSELF: What do we have that we're not using? Maybe it's data. Do you sit on interesting data that could be turned into a compelling report or infographic (think about how Spotify uses its listening data for the Wrapped campaign, turning user data into shareable stories)? Maybe it's customer passion, do you have die-hard fans you've never spotlighted? When I was at FreshBooks, we realized our small business customers were an asset themselves. We started promoting them, featuring their success stories, even creating fake "baseball cards" of our customers to hand out at events. That sounds crazy (promote other people instead of your product), but it worked because it built community and good-will; our customers became our evangelists. Their stories made others say "If FreshBooks works for them, maybe it'll work for me." All because we recognized our customer base as an under-leveraged asset for content and word-of-mouth.

MAYBE YOUR HIDDEN asset is a partnership opportunity. Who out there has something idle that you could use? Zipcar (where I worked pre-FreshBooks) had lots of cars sitting unused at certain times, we leveraged that to host events (like that rock concert we threw by bartering car access for a venue and bands). Empty cars became tickets to a memorable experience for customers, which became buzz. We traded driving credits for movie premier passes that we had contests with our users to win the passes and many other things. What does your company have sitting idle at night, on weekends, or in the metaphorical attic? Warehouse space that could become an art show venue? An email list that could become a networking circle if you connect the people on it? Excess product inventory that could be donated in a publicity-generating way (better than gathering dust)? An old blog with decent traffic that you could invite guest contributors to, turning it into a community platform? All banana stands of one sort or another.

SOMETIMES THE HIDDEN asset is your own personal quirk. I often inject my personality and absurd ideas into projects, that's an asset too. It differentiates my work. Don't shy away from what makes you or your brand unique, even if it's odd. Especially if it's odd! Odd can be a superpower. I've built a reputation as the guy who might show up at your event in a superhero costume or send you a cake with an edible marketing message on it. That's just "Saul being Saul," and it's helped me stand out in a field where a lot of people are polished but forgettable. In your case, maybe you have a hobby or skill unrelated to your business that could spark an original idea. Are you a musician? Maybe your next product demo should be a musical. Do you love retro video games? Maybe there's an 8-bit style Easter egg you could build into your website that delights users. Use all parts of the buffalo, including the weird parts.

A GREAT EXERCISE is to list out all your assets, tangible and intangible. Tangible: facilities, equipment, products, left-over materials, budget (or lack thereof, even lack of budget is a sort of "asset" in that it forces cheap innovation). Intangible: brand personality, team talents (e.g., do you have someone on staff who's secretly a stand-up comic or a TikTok star?), customer community, stories, core values, etc. Look at that list and ask, "Are we fully utilizing this? Could this be turned into a creative idea or experience?" You might be surprised. Sometimes a massive, game-changing idea is sitting right under your nose camouflaged as a mundane asset.

One of my favorite hidden asset stories (outside of my

own escapades) is how a small pizzeria once realized their delivery guys' cars were assets, the cars are out driving around town anyway, so why not turn them into moving billboards? They painted them into giant pizza slices. Cheesy (literally), but memorable. Or how a hotel with a nice rooftop realized they could host yoga classes at sunrise up there, something they'd never advertised, but it became a hit with guests once offered. The roof was always there; it just wasn't used creatively.

THE BANANA STAND was always there in the Arrested Development universe, full of cash, but the characters didn't realize it until they were desperate. Don't wait until you're desperate. Look around now with fresh eyes: What's your banana stand? Identify it, and you might find not only money there, but originality and differentiation.

And remember, using underused assets often ties back to constraints: you're leveraging what you do have because of what you don't have. That's the sweet spot for innovation. FreshBooks didn't have a huge ad budget, but we had a goofy idea and willingness to hustle, so we built that stand. That story still gets us love to this day (people like you reading about it in a book). The ROI of a creative idea built on a hidden asset can be massive and long-lasting.

So, go on a treasure hunt in your business or project. Make "banana stand" your code word for hidden gold. I promise, you have some, every organization does. Find it, dust it off, and see if you can turn it into your next big original idea.

BRINGING WoMBAT into Your Brainstorms

You might be thinking, "Alright, this sounds cool, but how do I actually do this with my team (or myself)?" Don't overcomplicate it. Next time you're facing a challenge, launching a product, fixing a customer experience, whatever, literally frame the problem as a WoMBAT question. Write it on the whiteboard: "What might be all the ways to [achieve X]?" Then go for quantity. No idea is too silly. In fact, the sillier the better at first. Don't discuss them, don't shoot anything down mid-stream. Just list every crazy "might be" idea you can.

Maybe you're brainstorming a new marketing campaign and someone says, "What if we print our message on the moon?" Sure, that's absurd, but instead of killing it, ask what kernel is interesting there. Is it the scale? The audacity? Maybe it inspires a more realistic idea like a projection on a city skyline. The point is, you got to that second idea by entertaining the insane first one.

I'VE SAT in countless ideation sessions where the first thing on the agenda is "What's our realistic budget and timeline?" That's like strangling the baby in the crib with the parents watching. Separate your imagination phase from your evaluation phase. WoMBAT is pure imagination phase. There's plenty of time later to apply filters and practicalities. And guess what, you'll still be more creative in execution because you aimed higher to begin with.

EVEN THE WORLD'S most innovative leaders do this. Hal Gregersen at MIT interviewed top CEOs and found their common trait was asking "catalytic questions" that transform the problem. These leaders give their teams freedom to explore the "What might be…" before narrowing down. So whether you're a team of one or one thousand, the principle holds.

Pro tip:

Encourage your team (or yourself) to frame multiple WoMBAT questions around the same problem, from different angles. In the Harlem example, we didn't stop at "ways to bring Harlem to life." We also asked "ways to show the soul of the show," "ways to tap forgotten details," etc.. Each phrasing pulls your mind in a new direction. It's like turning the Rubik's cube to see another face of the problem. You'll be amazed how a slight reframe, even just swapping verbs or targets in the question, can yield a totally different set of ideas.

EMBRACING Creative Bravery

Creative Bravery is one of the threads that run through all these stories. It's one thing to come up with a bold idea; it's another to sell it and execute it. Using WoMBAT will give you a bunch of daring ideas, but you have to have the guts to champion them. That might mean convincing a skeptical client, or your boss, or just yourself that it's worth taking a risk.

HERE'S MY TAKE: playing it safe is actually the riskiest move in the long run. In a world where consumers are bombarded with thousands of messages a day, nobody remembers the safe ideas. No one tweets about the 800th "official brand block party" they attended. But they'll remember the brand that did something crazy, fun, or deeply resonant. They'll remember the cloud software company that actually wrote messages in the sky (yes, I did that, we hired skywriters to promote a cloud computing firm). They'll remember the accounting software that toured the country handing out free hugs and waffles (guilty again).

THEY'LL REMEMBER a naked belt runway or a chance to loot a fake store or a comic book catalog. And that memory, that emotional reaction, is worth gold in marketing.

SO BE BRAVE. Ask the outrageous question. Propose the idea that gives you butterflies. What's the worst that can happen? A client says no? Okay. Move on to the next idea (or the next client). But if they say yes... if they embrace it... you just might create something legendary together.

And here's a secret: bravery is contagious. I've seen it with my clients. The first time you pitch a wild idea, they might balk. But maybe they compromise and do a tamer version, and it works better than they expected. Next time, they let you push a little further. After a few wins, they're the ones saying, "Alright, what crazy thing are we doing next quarter?" That evolution is awesome to watch. By using WoMBAT to constantly expand the idea landscape, you're not just coming up with one campaign, you're gradually shifting the culture of your team or client toward embracing creativity.

TO CIRCLE back to the beginning: How do I come up with my ideas? I *ask "What might be all the…?" and I don't stop until I've found the idea that makes all the normal ideas look lame by comparison. It's a simple habit, but it's unbelievably powerful. So go ahead, give it a try. Next time you're staring at a problem and feeling stuck, channel your inner WoMBAT. Ask a bigger question, a stranger question, a funnier question. You just might be surprised where your mind goes, and what brilliant, ballsy idea scurries out of its hiding spot.

Remember: Safe is average. Questions are free. And bold is where the magic is.

NOW… what might be all the ways you can apply this tomorrow?

YOUR CREATIVE CHEERLEADER (Go Forth and Find Ideas!)

We've covered a lot of ground in this chapter. By now you should feel armed with both inspiration and practical tools to generate original ideas even when "there's nothing new under the sun." We've debunked the notion that you need to be struck by genius; instead, you'll prime yourself for insights by connecting dots, relaxing your brain at times, and remembering that ideas are hiding everywhere around you. You know that humor isn't just a personality trait, it's a creative force multiplier (so maybe you have a scientific excuse to watch a few cat memes before your next brainstorming session, you know, for the sake of divergent thinking). You see constraints not as shackles, but as puzzles that spur inventive solutions, every constraint is a dare for you to do something clever. You have WoMBAT in your toolkit, ready to blast open the walls of any narrow question and let your imagination roam free on all the possibilities. You've got the improv mindset of "Yes, and" to keep the creative momentum, and you've learned the power of brainwriting to unlock the smarts of everyone on your team (including yourself). You won't hesitate to mix and mash unusual combos, because you know that's where some of the coolest innovations come from. And you'll never look at a "leftover" the same way again, whether it's empty seats, extra inventory, a quirk of your product, or heck, a pile of bananas, you'll ask "Could this be my secret weapon?"

NOW, I want to end on a personal note. I'm in your corner. Seriously. Imagine me as that slightly crazy friend in your head (the one who might show up with a truck full of bananas or suggest you jump over buses on a motorcycle) who genuinely believes in your creative potential. Because I do. I've seen too many "non-creative" people discover their creative mojo when given the right nudge, the right environment, or the right challenge. If you've read this far, you care about upping your creative game. And that means you've got what it takes. Creativity isn't some exclusive club talent; it's a muscle. You now have a whole workout regimen for it.

· · ·

NEXT TIME you're tasked with coming up with a campaign, a product idea, a solution to a big hairy problem, I want you to picture us in the bath together and hear me whisper (or shout) in your ear: "Go for the weird solution! Ask the big question! Use what you've got! What's the banana stand here?" and maybe "Have a laugh first!" Don't be afraid to be the one in the meeting who says something offbeat, that's the spark that might light the fire. Don't be afraid to iterate 50 ideas to get to the golden one, the research is on your side there (quantity leads to quality). And when you find that idea that makes you sit up and go "Wait… this just might work… and it's crazy enough that no one's tried it," I want you to feel the grin spreading on your face. That's when you know you've got something original.

REMEMBER, no new ideas doesn't mean no original ideas. Originality is within reach, because it's really about seeing the old with fresh eyes. It's about context, execution, and heart. Two people can have the same idea, but only one makes it original by the way they bring it to life with their unique spin. Be that person. Put you into it, your humor, your constraints, your questions, your hidden assets, your daring. That's something no one else can replicate.

I'LL LEAVE you with this: every time I've taken a wild creative leap, whether it was betting FreshBooks' conference budget on a banana stand stunt, or convincing a client to let us turn their promo video into a full-on musical, or driving across America to have meals with 2,000 customers, every time, I had butterflies in my stomach. Original ideas often feel scary because they are unproven. But those butterflies are a sign that you're onto something. And every single time, even if the idea didn't pan out exactly as imagined, it led to something good, buzz, learning, growth, another door opening. I've never regretted a bold idea. Not one. I have, however, regretted the times I held back and played it safe. So now, I err on the side of courage. I hope you will too...and I can't wait to see what brilliant, original things you'll do next. I'm cheering for you, loudly, with a banana in hand.

Class dismissed – now go make something awesome.

4 /
putting wombat to work.

WELCOME BACK, brave reader. By now you've met WoMBAT, our not-so-furry brainstorming friend, and you're itching to unleash it on the real world. This chapter is all about application: how to run a WoMBAT session, how to pry loose remarkable ideas in practice, and why you should stop waiting for some mythical lightning bolt of inspiration to strike.

Spoiler: Lightning is overrated, and curiosity (plus a dash of crazy) is far more reliable.

We'll walk through the ground rules of WoMBAT brainstorming, then dive into war stories from my career, paid cab rides, banana stands, BBQ buses, mimes, circus freaks, Air Sex (yes, that's a thing), all to show how asking better questions leads to outrageous, effective ideas. Along the way we'll shatter the creative myths that hold you back. No more sitting around hoping for the muse to show up. Instead, you'll learn to feed your brain the right inputs, embrace discomfort, remix what works, and make magic on demand. Buckle up (seatbelts save lives, especially on runaway marketing stunts). It's time to run with the WoMBAT.

. . .

THE WOMBAT WAY: Rules for Ridiculously Creative Brainstorms

Let's start with the WoMBAT method itself, the simple, CIA-approved framework for explosive ideation. To recap, WoMBAT stands for "What Might Be All The...", and it's all about reframing problems to unlock every possible solution. But a framework is only as good as its execution. Here are the ground rules I insist on whenever we run a WoMBAT session (write these on a flip chart, tattoo them on your forearm, whatever works):

Start with "What might be all the...?" Every brainstorm prompt must begin this way. This phrasing does psychological voodoo: it broadens your thinking and strips away judgment. If you ask, "How can we get more customers?" you'll get a few safe answers. But ask, "What might be all the ways to make our brand the most talked-about thing in accounting software?" and suddenly the floodgates open. WoMBAT questions free you to consider wild, "impossible" ideas, not just the obvious ones.

Timebox it (15–20 minutes max). Set a timer and go full throttle until the buzzer. Why a time limit? Because creativity loves pressure (just like diamonds). A short sprint forces your brain to outrun the inner critic. It's amazing how many ideas pop out in minute 19 that never would in an open-ended slog.

No judging, no filtering, no "Yeah, but...". In a WoMBAT blitz, every idea is a good idea for the next 20 minutes. Suspend all evaluation. If someone blurts out "We could hire a blimp and drop 10,000 marshmallows on Times Square," the only acceptable response is "Awesome, and what might be all the other airborne dessert drops we could do?" Off-the-wall suggestions often trigger the breakthrough, so embrace the absurd. Judgment can come later; during the brainstorm, the weirder the better.

Go for volume. This isn't the time to be precious. Crank

out as many ideas as humanly possible, dozens if you can. Don't stop to polish an idea, just get it out and move on. There's solid science behind this: Studies consistently show that the quantity of ideas leads to quality, because a bigger pool raises the odds of a brilliant one emerging.

Nobel laureate Linus Pauling put it best: "The best way to have a good idea is to have a lot of ideas."

So aim for a big pile of raw material.

After the sprint: Pick the ideas that make you feel something. Once the timer rings and your whiteboard looks like a beautiful mind's fever dream, then you can put on your editor's hat. Don't simply pick the most practical idea, pick the ones that make you laugh, think, or even cry (in a good way). These emotional reactions are gold. In my playbook I literally filter by "Laugh, Think, Cry." Why? Because if an idea cracks you up, blows your mind, or gives you goosebumps, it's likely to do the same for your audience. My personal formula is to ensure every marketing stunt hits at least two of the three notes, get a laugh, provoke thought, or tug the heartstrings. If it doesn't trigger any emotion in you, toss it. As a wise man (me) once summarized: Make your audience do two of three things, laugh, think, or cry. Ideas that spark emotion = ideas worth pursuing.

Follow these rules and you'll conduct a WoMBAT session that leaves your conference room littered with sticky notes full of outrageous possibilities. This process rewards curiosity over certainty – you're literally asking "What might be...?" instead of "What is the answer?", and it deliberately prioritizes imagination before constraints. You'll be shocked how often the best business strategy starts as a half-joke from the back of the room. Speaking of which, let's look at how some of those "half-jokes" turned into marketing legend.

BETTER QUESTIONS, Bigger Ideas: Hijacking a Trade Show (with Buses)

Allow me to set the scene: It's 2010, and FreshBooks (the scrappy online invoicing startup where I was known, only semi-ironically, as the "Head of Magic") is gearing up for a major industry conference so we held a free pancake breakfast in the parking lot to surprise bleary-eyed conventioneers. And remember those branded buses and cab rides you heard about? Here's the scoop: rather than pay for a booth, we paid for attendees' transportation, we literally shuttled people from the airport to their hotels saving them $40 and we go the opportunity to share all the wonders of FreshBooks. One rainy night at SXSW, I even hired a bus and invited 120 random festival-goers on a pilgrimage to a legendary BBQ joint outside Austin, all on FreshBooks' dime. We had a caravan of startups and creatives bonding over ribs and brisket at the Salt Lick Ranch, thanks to a simple question: "What might be all the ways to make a tech crowd happy in a downpour?" Answer: warm BBQ and a free ride. It was one of those shared experiences people never forget, and they certainly didn't forget FreshBooks after that.

Each of these stunts was born from curiosity and bold questions. None required a huge budget, just the willingness to zig while everyone else zagged. WoMBAT is a mindset, not just a tool, a willingness to ask "What if…?" and chase the interesting answers. When you reward curiosity over certainty, your marketing stops looking like marketing and starts feeling like an adventure.

NO MAGIC SPARKS

Now let's address the woolly mammoth in the room: the myth of creative inspiration. You know, the idea that big ideas arrive in a flash of genius, bestowed by the muse while you're soaking in the bathtub (hey, Archimedes) or lounging under an apple tree (nice one, Newton). So many people wait for that divine spark, which is about as reliable as waiting for actual lightning in a bottle. Time for some tough love: creative lightning bolts are B.S. The professionals don't sit around praying for Zeus to zap them; they're too busy working the process.

In fact, *58% of people still believe that creative achievements are usually the result of a sudden inspiration.*

More than half of us think great ideas just pop out of thin air in a brilliant aha! moment. No wonder folks imagine creativity as this mystical hit-or-miss thing. But here's the unromantic truth: those "overnight epiphanies" are usually the result of hours, days, or years of input and subconscious processing, the part nobody sees. As Psychology Today put it, the eureka moments of Newton and Archimedes didn't magically manifest; "the seeds for those ideas had already been planted , they just needed time to germinate." In other words, the "lightning bolt" is really just your brain connecting dots you've been feeding it all along.

Why is the lightning myth so dangerous? Because it tricks you into waiting. If you think you need to feel inspired first, you'll sit on your hands forever. You'll say, "Nah, nothing's coming to me today, maybe tomorrow I'll have my big idea," meanwhile your competition is out there generating a hundred ideas, testing 99 bad ones, and implementing the one good one. The truth is, creativity is an action, not a mood. You don't wait to feel creative, you do the work and become creative. I often tell people: Inspiration is for amateurs. The rest of us have a system. And that system is all about inputs and pattern recognition.

Think of your brain as a web of neurons just waiting to form new connections. The more raw material you throw in, stories, facts, experiences, random bits of trivia, the more connections it can make. Over time, those connections can crystallize into an "aha!" idea. It's not magic; it's associative thinking. Researchers have long noted that creativity is basically connecting concepts in novel ways. In fact, a 2023 study in Trends in Cognitive Sciences affirmed that "creativity has long been thought to involve associative processes in memory: connecting concepts to form ideas, inventions, and artworks.". Creative people aren't lightning rods, they're collectors and combiners. They pile up tons of curious inputs, then their brains remix them below conscious awareness, and eventually out pops something "new".

As the neuroscientist David Eagleman explained, when you finally get an idea, your brain's been working behind the scenes on it for a long time, "trying out new combinations" of all the stuff you've taken in.

So if you want more creative ideas, don't pray for lightning, go play in the rain. Expose yourself to diverse inputs, fill your head with knowledge and experiences (especially outside your industry), and practice divergent thinking. Divergent thinking is just a ten-dollar term for the ability to generate lots of ideas or solutions, and it's a muscle you can strengthen. A habit of divergent thinking naturally leads to a quantity of ideas, and as we established, that's the precursor to quality. In one charming experiment recounted in art circles, a pottery teacher split students into two groups: one had to make one perfect pot, the other had to make as many pots as possible. The quantity group churned out pot after pot, learning from each one, and by the end they had produced far better work than the single-pot perfectionists. The moral: chaos, messes, and dozens of "okay" ideas pave the way to the showstopper. It's a process of elimination and iteration. Even geniuses like Edison knew this, he famously said, "I haven't failed, I've just found 9,000 ways that won't work." The lightbulb wasn't a thunderbolt of inspiration; it was brute-force trial and error.

Don't just take it from me and old dead inventors. Modern research backs this up with hard data. Creativity scholars call it "blind variation and selective retention", which is fancy talk for generate lots of variations, then select the best. Also, personalities who are high in novelty-seeking (the kind of people who chase new experiences and information) tend to score higher in divergent thinking and creative output. One 2019 study found that actively encouraging a novelty-seeking mindset led to greater divergent thinking performance. In plain English: if you cultivate curiosity and a taste for new things, you'll come up with more ideas. It's that simple. (Side note: this is why WoMBAT works so well, it literally forces you to consider novel angles and prevents you from settling on the first "normal" idea.)

In our WoMBAT sessions at The Idea Integration Co., I've watched this play out time and again. The first few ideas people offer are usually the safe, obvious ones (the brain's warm-up). But by idea 37, someone throws in a curveball that came from who-knows-where, perhaps some random documentary they watched or a hobby they have, and that's the one that makes the room gasp, "Hold on, that one… that's interesting." Those brilliant ideas aren't bolts from the blue; they're the fruits of cross-pollination and persistence. We didn't wait for them, we went digging.

To sum up: Reject the lightning bolt myth. Don't sit in the dark waiting for illumination. Instead, turn on a floodlight and start actively exploring. Ask a WoMBAT question and list out 50 answers. Read weird stuff. Talk to people outside your field. Embrace the mindset that ideas are out there, ripe to be recognized, not hiding in some divine cloud. As one Psychology Today article noted, "we often embrace the myth of a strike of inspiration... as a result, we wait in vain", when really "creativity is an action, not a feeling." So go take action. The muse favors the busy.

THE WOMBAT MINDSET: Curiosity Over Certainty

One of the biggest shifts you'll feel when you adopt WoMBAT thinking is a sense of childlike curiosity returning to your work. Instead of fretting, "What's the correct solution?" you'll find yourself wondering, "What if we tried this? And what about that?" Questions become more valuable than answers. This is a profound change from how most of us operate in business. We're trained to exude confidence and certainty, have a plan, know the plan, execute the plan. But certainty can be a creativity killer. If you're sure you know how something is done, you won't look for better ways. Certainty puts blinders on you; curiosity rips them off.

Research shows that curiosity is a powerful driver of creativity. One review of studies in late 2023 concluded that "curiosity enhances creativity" and can even boost enthusiasm and engagement at work. When you're curious, you're more likely to tinker, to explore unorthodox ideas, and to persist in the face of uncertainty (because, heck, you want to see what will happen). WoMBAT is essentially formalized curiosity. It rewards asking "Why? Why not? What if?" at every turn.

In my career, the times I've been praised for "vision" or "innovation," I swear I was just asking a lot of questions and not pretending to have all the answers. WoMBAT turns this into a habit. It institutionalizes wonder. And guess what, fostering a culture of curiosity can transform a whole team. When people aren't afraid to raise a wild question in a meeting, you start getting far more interesting discussions. I've seen junior employees stun a room with a question that upends our assumptions and unlocks a huge idea. That only happens when leaders encourage curiosity over the illusion of always being right.

Curiosity also means being willing to not know and to learn. It's about listening as much as talking. Some of the best WoMBAT questions are ones that seek input rather than spout expertise. For example, when Freshii (the healthy fast-food chain) wanted to make a splash, instead of just declaring "We're going to beat McDonalds with salads!" they got curious: "What might be all the ways to get on McDonalds radar without a huge ad budget?" The answer they landed on was bold: an open letter from Freshii's CEO to McDonalds, published as a full-page newspaper "open letter", basically saying "Hey McDonalds, people want fresher things so let's partner up and convert a small portion of all your locations into Freshii locations so people can get fresh salads and fries." Audacious? Absolutely. It got tons of press. Freshii didn't quietly try to compete; they curiously posed a win-win scenario to a rival in a very public way. That's WoMBAT thinking: ask a question that makes people stop and think ("Could two competitors actually help each other?"). In reality, McDonalds didn't take them up on it, but Freshii won attention and framed themselves as a creative, collaborative upstart. They made us think, which as you know is one of the golden emotions to hit…and if you are wondering where this idea came from it is a take off of the episode of Mad Men where they took a full page ad out to say they will no longer work with tobacco brands. #nonewideas

Curiosity also means comfort with not having the immediate answer. A WoMBAT mindset in a company means brainstorming possible futures rather than insisting on one forecast. It's scenario planning, something even the CIA uses WoMBAT for, as we noted. The CIA! If the folks handling national security threats can admit "We don't know the answer, so let's map out all the possibilities," your marketing team can certainly say "Let's explore all the ways this campaign could go" instead of fixating on one safe idea.

Bottom line: Curiosity keeps you searching and discovering, which keeps you innovative. Certainty just makes you stagnant and often wrong. So stay curious. Ask the extra question. Hell, ask stupid questions, sometimes those open the smartest doors. Be the person in the meeting who says, "I know this might sound crazy, but what if…?" That phrase is the anthem of the WoMBAT mindset. I've built a career on starting sentences with "This might be crazy, but…". Nine times out of ten the answer is, "Yeah, Saul, that's pretty crazy." But on the tenth time, it's pure gold.

TALES FROM THE TRENCHES: Parties, Pranks, and WTF Moments

Enough theory , let's get into some juicy stories. I've been called sexy, infamous and even notorious (among other colorful adjectives) for the stunts and word-of-mouth campaigns I've pulled off. The goal is always strategic , get people talking and emotionally engaged with a brand, but the tactics often look more like performance art or comedy sketches than "marketing." I do this intentionally, because memorable = shareable. If you want true word-of-mouth, you have to give 'em a story worth sharing around the digital campfire. Here are a few of my greatest hits (and a couple near-misses) that show WoMBAT in action:

FreshBooks "Tupperware" Parties – Making Accounting Fun at Home

When I was at FreshBooks, we realized we had passionate users who loved the product. So we thought, why not bring them together? We borrowed a page from the old Tupperware party model. Yes, those 1950s house parties where someone sells plastic containers in your living room. We asked, "What might be all the ways to turn our customers into evangelists?" One way: throw them a party! We equipped a few super-fan customers with kits to host gatherings for fellow small business owners, we're talking pizza, beer, and a casual demo of FreshBooks in someone's backyard or apartment. No hard sell, just peers sharing cool software. These were essentially FreshBooks house parties, low-key, fun, and community-driven, like friends showing friends a new tool. They felt authentic because they were; it was customers spreading the word, not corporate suits. Those parties led to new signups and, more importantly, stronger customer relationships. We didn't have to beg people to talk about FreshBooks, we gave them a social excuse to do it. And unlike a sterile demo in a fluorescent-lit office, this was accounting software pitched between bites of BBQ and beers, with laughter in the air. (Rule of thumb: If you can associate your brand with good food and good times, do it.)

GUERRILLA THEATRE: Mimes, Freak Shows, and Air Sex – Oh My!

Confession: I love the circus. Ringling Bros style and the weird stuff: sideshows, shock comedians, performance art.

Why? Because it surprises people and evokes raw reactions, you laugh, you gasp, you cover your eyes. Early in my career, I realized those are exactly the responses I want in marketing. So I thought, what might be all the ways to inject that WTF-factor into brand events?

For one tech networking event, I hired a mime to work the crowd. Yup, a classic French mime with white facepaint, silently wandering through a sea of chatty sales reps. At first people were perplexed ("Who invited Marcel Marceau over here?"). But soon, the mime became the unofficial mascot of the event, folks were taking selfies pretending to be trapped in his invisible box, following his exaggerated pointing to find the bar, etc. It created a shared joke that broke the ice among attendees. Strangers laughed together at the absurdity of a mime handing them a business card with an exaggerated flourish (yes, I had him give out FreshBooks cards without saying a word). It was irreverent and weird, but it made that networking night unforgettable. Instead of another dull exchange of LinkedIn info, people had a story: "Remember that conference with the mime? And how he crashed the fintech mixer?" By making everyone a little uncomfortable at first, we actually brought them closer together by the end. Discomfort can be bonding when it turns into laughter.

Now, if a mime is mildly weird, the Jim Rose Circus Sideshow is extremely weird. Jim Rose, for the uninitiated, is a legendary performer who does outrageous stunts, think human blockheads, sword swallowers, people hanging weights from delicate body parts (yes we are hinting at genitals). I had the crazy idea once to mash up a tech product launch with a Jim Rose-style freak show. Why? Because a typical product launch is boring as hell. No one remembers what hapless exec droned on stage about "disruption" last week. But you bet they'll remember if during that launch a man is juggling chainsaws or lying on a bed of nails promoting your slogan. So we did it, we put on a mini sideshow extravaganza alongside the corporate event. Did it make some people squeamish? Sure. But they couldn't stop talking about it. That brand instantly stood out as daring and different. It whispered to the audience: "We're not like the others, we've got guts (and maybe a twisted sense of humor)." That emotional imprint, equal parts "haha" and "holy crap" – is marketing gold. It made them laugh and cringe (which is basically a cousin of crying), two emotional triggers in one.

And then… there's Air Sex. If you've never heard of it, Air Sex Championships are exactly what they sound like: imagine an Air Guitar contest, but instead of pretending to play guitar, contestants… er… simulate amorous encounters with invisible partners, on stage, fully clothed but utterly ridiculous. It's part comedy, part… I don't know, performance art? In any case, it's bizarre and hysterical. Naturally, I thought this would be a great side event at a conference. So we hosted an Air Sex Championship as a sponsored event for a client. The brand tie-in was subtle (this wasn't porn, folks, it was comedy, absurd overacting, not actual lewdness), but the key was associating our client with an outrageous fun time. Picture a ballroom full of startup founders and investors, unwinding after a day of panels by watching something between improv comedy and a fake orgasm contest. People were crying laughing. The client's logo was on the step-and-repeat behind the stage, on the event tickets, etc., forever linked to that memorable night. We turned a staid business conference into something borderline insane, and everyone loved it. Next day, it's all they could talk about in the hallways: "Did you see the Air Sex last night? That was sponsored by WHO? What do they do?!" Mission accomplished: curiosity ignited. That brand suddenly had an edgy, fun aura. And it cost us maybe a few thousand bucks in event costs, far less than any forgettable sponsored lunch or banner ad everyone ignores.

Now, a word of caution: these kinds of stunts must fit the brand's personality or desired image. Not every company should align itself with mimes and freak shows and simulated nookie. But when it does make sense (or when you want to signal a maverick personality), go all in. Don't half-ass the weirdness. The reason these worked is because we committed, we didn't just sprinkle a tiny bit of odd; we drenched the audience in it so they couldn't ignore it.

The through-line in all these tales is that emotion and

surprise beat rational appeals every time. If we had just given people a 20% off coupon, would they remember? No. But the human brain never forgets a strong emotional experience, whether it's laughter, shock, or awe. Neuroscience 101: emotion cements memory. That's why I design marketing like an entertainer or showman. It's not "stunts for stunts' sake", it's strategy for capturing mindshare. As one article about word-of-mouth noted, "unforgettable moments and experiences are what really get people talking". People share stories that surprise or delight them, not stories that are "pretty normal, nothing to see here."

LEARNING to Love the Creative Squeeze: Why Friction and Discomfort Spark Innovation

By now you might be thinking, "Okay Saul, you clearly aren't afraid to make people uncomfortable. But is that really necessary for creativity?" My answer: YES, at least, in the right ways. Let's talk about discomfort and friction in creative work. There's a psychological phenomenon called cognitive disfluency, basically, when something is a bit hard to process, it forces you to slow down and think more deeply. Believe it or not, studies have found disfluency can lead to better outcomes in certain tasks because it shakes you out of autopilot. For example, one experiment showed that when students read text in a slightly harder-to-read font, they retained more information, because they had to pay closer attention. Struggle a little, learn a lot.

I apply this insight to brainstorming and culture. If everyone in the room agrees readily and nods along, you're likely not exploring truly new territory. It's too fluent, too easy. But introduce a bit of friction, a dissenting opinion, a wild idea that makes people squirm, and suddenly the mind has to engage more deeply. You get off the beaten path. I intentionally create "cognitive disfluency" in ideation by asking oddball questions or bringing in an outside perspective with no context (forcing the team to explain everything from scratch). It may feel awkward or like extra work, but it jolts us into creativity. Disfluency "prompts people to process information more carefully, deeply, and abstractly", which is exactly what you need for breakthrough ideas.

The same goes for comfort zones in general. We all know innovation dies in echo chambers and yes-men environments. If your team is homogeneous and always in agreement, I guarantee you're leaving brilliant ideas on the table. A 2017 survey of creative professionals found that most felt they were stuck in an "echo chamber" with insufficient diverse views. They worried this was "warping creativity", and they're right. If everyone around you thinks alike, your ideas will be variations of the same theme. It's like playing tennis against a wall, predictable and unchallenging. Diversity of thought, and even constructive conflict, is the friction that strikes creative sparks. When I brainstorm, I want people with different backgrounds, I want healthy debate, I even want someone to say "This idea makes me uncomfortable" because then we can dig into why, and often that why reveals a deeper insight.

Take the earlier example of the freak show product launch. Internally, that idea wasn't immediately embraced by all. Some execs said "Are you nuts? That's off-brand. We can't do that." That discomfort was actually useful, it forced us to clarify the purpose and ensure the stunt tied into brand message in the right way. We fine-tuned the execution to balance shock and relevance. The little battle made the idea stronger. And ultimately, crossing that line (business + circus sideshow = 😶) was what made it memorable.

ONE OF MY MANTRAS IS: "If you don't cross the line, you're not making memories... Being forgotten is the worst thing a brand could be.".". A bit of risk, a bit of discomfort, signals you're doing something novel. Of course, you have to gauge the risk, I'm not saying be offensive or reckless for no reason. But I am saying that if no one on your team is at least a tad nervous about a campaign, it's probably too safe to matter.

Psychologists also talk about the mere-exposure effect, basically we like things just because they're familiar. That's fine for selling soft drinks maybe, but in creative work it's a trap. If you only stick with what everyone's seen a million times, you'll bore your audience. Familiarity breeds complacency. I prefer the mischief effect (I just made that up): doing something a bit unfamiliar, a bit challenging, so that people snap out of their trance. For instance, no one expected a financial software company to throw a wild party or send them a goofy piece of direct mail. We leaned into that incongruity. One time at FreshBooks we mailed out actual sandwiches to a few top prospects with a note like "Let's do lunch (on us), call me!" It was a refrigerated sub in a box delivered to their office. Talk about pattern interrupt! Did some recipients find it odd? Sure. But did it get attention and start conversations? You bet (some called just to ask "Why the hell did you send me a sandwich?", to which we said "Because we really want a chance to show you FreshBooks, and hey, free lunch!"). It broke the echo chamber of boring B2B sales outreach, and that's why it worked.

The point is, a little discomfort can be extremely productive. It keeps you on your toes. It makes you question assumptions. It gets your brain out of ruts and into gear. Creative environments shouldn't feel like a warm bath; they should feel like a brisk splash of cold water. Not full-on torture, mind you, just enough challenge to wake everyone up.

So don't be afraid to introduce creative tension. Argue the opposite of your own idea to test it. Invite that oddball colleague to your planning session. Try brainstorming in a new environment (like, take the team to an improv class or an art studio for a day, I've done both; it weirded people out at first, then yielded awesome ideas). If things get too comfy, disrupt it. Remember, friction can either wear you down or polish you into a shine, it all depends on how you use it. We choose to use it to shine.

STEAL THE STRUCTURE, Not the Story: How to Remix Ideas Like a Pro

Let's address a subtle but important aspect of creativity: originality. People often worry, "Is my idea truly original, or am I just copying someone?" There's a famous saying (variously attributed to Picasso, T.S. Eliot, even Steve Jobs) that "Good artists copy; great artists steal." I prefer to phrase it as: Great innovators steal structures, not exact ideas. They remix and reassemble pieces from elsewhere into something fresh. Combinatorial creativity is the fancy term, virtually all new ideas are combinations of existing ones.

The key is not to plagiarize someone's content, but to borrow the underlying framework and give it your own twist. For example, when we did the banana stand, were we the first to ever do a pop-culture themed booth? Nope. We essentially "stole" the structure of a beloved TV gag and repurposed it for marketing. That's fair game, we weren't claiming we invented the Banana Stand, we were using it in a new context. People appreciated the reference, in fact it endeared us to them ("Haha, I love that show!"). Similarly, Freshii's open letter wasn't the first open letter stunt in advertising (brands have done cheeky letters before), but it was novel in context and content. We lifted the format and infused it with our own message.

There's a great concept in writing: "formulas" vs content. You can borrow a formula (say, the hero's journey narrative, or the open-letter format, or the viral challenge format) and plug in your own content to make it new. I do this consciously. I keep swipe files of cool campaigns, not to rip them off verbatim, but to examine why they worked and how I might adapt the mechanics. Did some other company create a citywide scavenger hunt that got huge engagement? Interesting, what might be all the ways we could do a scavenger hunt for our brand? Boom, now you're "stealing" the structure (scavenger hunt + community + reward) but the specifics are yours (perhaps clues related to your product, different city, different prize).

Creative remixing is how humanity has always progressed. Mark Twain said it best over a century ago: "Substantially all ideas are second-hand... the only thing that gives them value is a new arrangement.". I live by that. So I encourage you: be a student of remarkable ideas in any field, and figure out their structure. Then steal that and reassemble it for your needs. It's not cheating; it's smart. What's cheating is copying an idea note-for-note, that usually fails anyway, because context differs. But learning from an idea's architecture – that's just standing on the shoulders of giants.

A concrete example: We once looked at the dollar shave club viral video (you know, the hilarious "Our Blades Are Fucking Great" video that I keep mentioning like they are the only one who has ever done anything interesting) and thought, damn that tone and shock value made them a household name overnight. We didn't want to copy their jokes, but we did ask "What might be all the ways to apply that irreverent, blunt style to something as dry as accounting software?" That led to us producing a series of short videos for Xero (another accounting platform I worked with) where we had a comedian doing man-on-the-street interviews asking people ridiculously direct questions about their finances and making it funny. It wasn't as raunchy as Dollar Shave's, but it had that spirit of irreverence. It worked, people shared it saying "LOL

I can't believe an accounting company said that." We owed a tip of the hat to Dollar Shave's structure (humor + shock + low-budget authenticity), but the content was uniquely ours (nobody else would have asked a Brooklyn hipster if he writes off his beard oil as a business expense, trust me).

Here's another: I was inspired by Red Bull's insane stunts (like Felix Baumgartner's space jump). Obviously, a small brand can't do something of that scale. But we dissected it: what's the structure? A daredevil + a record-breaking feat + streaming it live + tying it loosely to the product (Red Bull gives you wings, get it). So for a much smaller client (a cigar company), we asked, "What might be all the ways to create a daredevil spectacle on a budget, to show this cigar is bold?" We sketched out an idea to have a pro climber scale the side of the client's office building and light a cigar on the roof – a nod to a famous urban climber nicknamed "French Spider-Man" who free-climbs skyscrapers. It was thrilling, symbolic (cigar at the top = victory smoke), and would generate press and killer visuals. We planned it out in detail, even got the daredevil on standby, ready to go.

Now, that particular idea… ahem… never saw the light of day (more on that later). The client loved it in theory, then got cold feet. The legal team probably had kittens imagining the liability, and the executives just weren't ready to be that brave. And you know what? That's okay. Not every crazy idea will fly (or climb). Sometimes creative ideas outpace the client's risk tolerance. We had to respect that. But I don't consider it a failure at all. The process of pitching a wild idea and talking it through helped the client clarify their comfort zone. We dialed it back and did a tamer campaign in the end. Did it set the world on fire? No. (To be honest, I still think our idea would have gotten them on the front page of the news… but I digress). The lesson: be willing to generate and present ideas that might be "too much." Pushing the boundary is how you find the line. If you never propose something that scares your client (or yourself), you're probably nowhere near an idea that will truly get noticed. As the saying goes, if you're not pissing someone off, you're not doing it right.

Also, even unrealized ideas add to your creative repertoire. Our cigar-climbing stunt was essentially "Evel Knievel meets corporate PR." Maybe it was too spicy for that cigar brand, but guess what, I have that concept filed away. Someday, for a bolder client or a different context, I might revive it.

Creativity is a long game. Today's "too crazy" idea could be tomorrow's brilliant plan for someone else. So never toss an idea completely; save it, tweak it, repurpose it down the line.

The art of stealing structure also means studying failures, yours and others'. If a competitor tried a stunt that flopped, analyze it. Was the structure sound but the execution off? Maybe you can do it right. If we had more time, I'd tell you about the time I mailed hundreds of whoopee cushions to journalists thinking it would get us press (structure: funny gag gift + press kit). It... didn't work as intended. But it taught me how to better target outreach (and that some reporters lack a sense of humor, their loss, honestly). We remixed that approach later by sending personalized humorous gifts rather than a one-size-fits-all whoopee, and got a much better result. Tweak the formula and try again.

To conclude this section: Originality is often overrated. In the quest for a "never-seen-before" idea, you can paralyze yourself. Instead, give yourself permission to build on existing ideas in novel ways. Creativity is more synthesis than genesis, you're combining old elements into a new whole. Once you internalize that, you'll feel a lot freer. You'll swipe structures from outside your industry, cross-pollinate concepts, and come up with stuff that feels completely original to your audience (who cares if it was inspired by a random thing you saw on YouTube?). Stealing like an artist, or a marketer, is about honorably borrowing and transforming. Do it with a wink and your own flair, and you'll never run out of fresh ideas.

CLOSING THOUGHTS: Embrace the WoMBAT, Become the WoMBAT

As we wrap up Chapter Four, I hope one thing is blazingly clear: WoMBAT isn't just a one-time brainstorming trick, it's a philosophy of how to approach creative challenges. It says that the answers are out there, but you have to ask the right crazy questions first. It says that ideas are born from active pursuit, not passive waiting. And it says that to get remarkable results, you must be willing to be a bit unreasonable.

We've covered a lot: how to run a WoMBAT session with reckless creative abandon, how FreshBooks turned a $500 idea into a conference showstopper, how Freshii turned a letter into a national conversation, how I've used everything from mimes to Air Sex to make brands unforgettable, and why none of this is as random as it sounds, it's grounded in strategy and some pretty nifty science about how humans think, share, and remember. We debunked the myth of the lightning bolt and replaced it with the reality of steady sparks and diligent kindling. We championed curiosity and discomfort as unlikely heroes of innovation. And we learned that stealing (when done with brains and style) is an essential part of creating.

If your head is spinning, that's okay. (Better than it nodding off, right?) Creativity is messy and nonlinear. But that's the beauty of the WoMBAT mindset, it thrives in chaos. It wants you to throw everything on the wall and see what sticks, to be silly and serious and bold and skeptical all at once. It's the opposite of the mythical lone genius waiting peacefully for a muse. It's more like a mad scientist's lab where something's always bubbling over. And from that frothy concoction, boom, you distill the magic.

I want you to feel empowered to try this. Host that WoMBAT session. Ask the wild question no one's asking. Maybe your boss will think you've lost it (until the results come in). Maybe you'll scare yourself a little with how far off the map you go. Good. Do it. Use the research in this chapter to back yourself up if anyone questions your methods. ("Actually, boss, science says curiosity boosts creativity and 58% of people believe in sudden inspiration but they're wrong, so we're doing this my way.") Then invite them to the party, literally or figuratively.

Remember, being a WoMBAT warrior is about mindset as much as technique. Reward your own curiosity. When you find yourself in a rut, ask "What might be all the reasons I'm stuck and all the ways I could get unstuck?" (WoMBAT works on oneself too!). When a "meh" idea is presented, challenge it with "What might be all the ways to make that idea crazier/bigger/more emotional?" Get used to the language of expansive thinking. It will become second nature.

And for heaven's sake, have fun with this. One thing I hope comes through in my stories is that I freaking love this stuff. Brainstorming is play for me, and it can be for you. There's a certain giddy thrill in doing what others don't expect, in crafting marketing that feels like a prank or a party or a piece of art. When you have fun, your audience can tell, and they join in. As a marketer or creator, you are an entertainer at heart, no matter your industry. Never forget that. Aim to entertain, delight, provoke, and you'll cut through the noise every time. As I often say, if people aren't talking about you, you've failed, because invisibility is death in branding. The worst outcome is not that some uptight person hated your stunt; the worst outcome is nobody noticed it at all. So dare to be noticed.

I'll leave you with this: The world is already full of boring ideas. It doesn't need another. It needs yours, the one only you could come up with because of your unique mix of experiences and inputs. To extract that idea, you have the tools now: WoMBAT questions, a mindset of curiosity, a tolerance for discomfort, and a willingness to remix and reimagine structures. You don't need a lightning bolt. You just need to start rubbing sticks together with a grin on your face, trusting that you'll spark a flame.

Alright, that's enough rah-rah from me. You've got the know-how; now go make some trouble. In the next chapter, we'll delve into how to actually run a WoMBAT brainstorm session. But for now, your mission is clear: unleash your inner WoMBAT and make your marketing worth talking about. The magic isn't in waiting, it's in the doing. So get out there and do. I can't wait to hear the stories you'll tell.

(Cue mic drop, and perhaps a man in a cape climbing a building in the distance... but that's another chapter.)

5 /
wombat, how to run a brainstorming session like a badass

SO YOU WANT ideas that aren't safe like a paper napkin, the kind that make people spit out their coffee and say "Holy shit, that's genius." Good. Welcome to WoMBAT, short for "What Might Be All The...", (i said I would keep reminding you) our top-secret CIA-inspired brainstorming playbook. If you've been stuck in yawn-fests where the best idea is a vanilla cupcake, you're in the right place. We're going to tear up the old rulebook and show you how to unleash creativity the Saul Colt way: loud, proud, and hilarious. Buckle up, buttercup , we're diving into the five steps to run a WoMBAT session that'll leave safe, boring ideas dazed and confused on the floor.

FRAME THE QUESTION Right

Ever start a brainstorm with "What should we do for blank?" Yawn. That question is like shooting flies with a water pistol: it barely scratches the surface. In WoMBAT, step one is to slap that lame question upside the head and reframe it. Turn it into a wide-open challenge by adding a sprinkle of "might," a dash of curiosity, and maybe even a touch of insanity. Instead of "How do we launch this new product?", try "What might be all the crazy ways to launch this new product?" See the difference? You just swapped a death sentence for your creativity with a neon-lit invitation to brainstorm like a maniac.

THIS TRICK IS magic because of framing bias , basically, your brain's annoying habit of fixating on the obvious problem instead of seeing the bigger picture. Imagine you're playing Where's Waldo? and you only stare at the picture. You might find Waldo, sure, but you'll totally miss the topless woman in the corner getting her hair done. (True story, happened in a classic Waldo puzzle.) If we treat business problems the same way, we miss giant, hilarious hippos of opportunity hiding in the margins. WoMBAT shoves Waldo aside and asks, "What if Waldo is hiding in a cloud of confetti or taking a nap on the moon?" Suddenly the game is infinitely more fun and you discover waldo-themed yacht parties or whatever crazy, cool stuff you wouldn't have even imagined before.

REAL TALK: framing the question right is half the battle. I told you about the time we pitched ideas for a nostalgia-heavy TV show set in 1970's Harlem. The client's early ideas were as safe as decaf coffee: block parties, club nights, a cocktail named after a character. Boring. I smelled cupcakes and I wanted steak. So we WoMBAT-ed the crap out of it: "What might be all the ways to bring real Harlem vibes to life?" Boom. Now the team was thinking beyond the flipchart, into the gritty, funky soul. (And yes, we eventually sketched out something involving actual street art, old-school jazz in parking lots, and maybe even a cameo from a legendary Harlem barber for a live haircut demo. Real wild stuff.)

Pro Tip: Use open-ended phrases. Don't say "good," say "what's all the bad, good, stupid, brilliant ways this might happen?" The wilder the question, the wilder (and potentially better) the answers. Think like a 5-year-old on sugar, not a corporate banker on decaf. In WoMBAT sessions, every question is an excuse to ask more questions. You're not looking for "the answer," you're looking for all the answers , even the ones your competitors haven't dreamt up yet.

SET the Stage

Before your team starts firing off ideas, create a playground, not a boardroom. Think less "starchy, fluorescent lights, please don't rock the boat," and more "We're about to light a bonfire of creativity here, bring marshmallows." Seriously, the vibe matters. If people feel like they're about to get crucified for saying something dumb, they'll stay quiet. If they feel like they're on SNL, saying the next off-the-wall line might make them a cult hero , well, that's where the magic happens.

HERE'S THE DEAL: Scrub the agenda. Ban all distractions like "budget constraints" and "SEO rankings" from earshot until after the brainstorm. Clear the room (literally). Bring in props or visuals to spark weird thoughts. I once turned our office into a belt-upholstery fashion house (no, really). We had models sashaying around with belts as clothes, think "Project Runway" meets utilitarian chic. Why? To remind everyone that sometimes you have to wear something stupid before you can invent the next great fashion trend. That little stunt, later affectionately called the "Fashion Belt Show," was pure theater and it loosened up the crew to scream out ideas like belt-shaped burritos or belt-sandwich presses (still love that one).

ANOTHER TIME AT SXSW, we equipped (another) RV and made it a rolling TV studio conducting interviews with the most interesting people at the conference. The RV was an also a moving billboard and our content made a real impact on people where the videos were getting watched in record numbers and people were begging to be featured in our "studio". This idea would have never come to reality in a traditional environment.

YOU HAVE to make it safe to be stupid. Have a no-judgment rule plastered on a poster so big no one can ignore it. Bring snacks (nothing kills creativity like hangry faces). Play some music , the more danceable, the better , to keep energy up. If it feels like a party or a jam session, you'll pull noise out of people's heads that normally sits in the "too crazy" drawer. Put a gold star on anyone who blurts something absurdly off-the-wall. (No, seriously. One session I had a trophy for "Best Outrageous Idea" , a tiny plastic giraffe painted gold. People went nuts for it.)

Remember: your environment whispers ideas to the group. If your walls are grey and your chairs are stiff, you'll get grey, stiff ideas. But if you let people stand on tables with superhero capes on, suddenly suggestions start looking like graphic novel panels. (I'm half-kidding. Mostly.)

GO for Volume (Not Genius)

Now the fun begins: spit everything out. Not just one or

two gleaming pearls , hundreds of turds and diamonds alike. This is the brainstorm equivalent of dumping an entire spice rack into the stew. Our aim? More ideas than a cat has lives. Because here's the dirty secret: the first ten ideas will be absolute dogshit. But buried somewhere after idea #47, there's often a nugget that shines.

ANNOUNCE A QUOTA: "I want 100 ideas in 15 minutes." Watch the panic and adrenaline mingle on faces. Those half-baked, jotted-on-a-napkin scribbles are pure gold because one of them is the silicon in your future rocket ship. And don't just sit around; shake your brain until it coughs up ideas. Techniques: do lightning rounds, scribble on Post-its, draw doodles, or even pipe it like a game show ("Name that idea!"). I've thrown out ideas like launching a mobile cloud in a meth lab, wearing frog costumes in Times Square, or writing press releases in iambic pentameter , just to keep the ball bouncing.

Pro tip: Push for obscene quantities. And I mean obscene. If a teammate says, "I'm tired, I have nothing," respond with, "Bullshit. Your brain is like a party animal with ADHD , there's always more where that came from!" It's amazing how competitive people get. Once you say "whoever writes more ideas in 3 minutes gets an awkwardly long hug from the boss," (we have no sexual harassment policy for this exact reason) ideas start spilling. We once gamified it so hard that someone whipped out a thesaurus and started combining unrelated words (result: "cottoneconomics" , no clue what it meant, but it was funny).

. . .

DON'T JUDGE. Not even internally. Write down the dumbest, most horrific suggestion on the wall right next to the brilliant ones. ("Tie marketing to ASMR videos of clouds reading copy." Fine, we wrote it down.) Why? Because your brain is sloppy. It'll throw out baby and bathwater if you say "No, that's dumb." Embrace the dumb. That's where creativity often hides.

EXAMPLE TIME: For a cloud-based accounting client, we needed a stunt. We brainstormed every single thing related to "cloud": actual clouds, pillows, weather patterns, head-in-the-clouds. We ended up with stuff like "cloud costume for a CEO," "cloud-shaped hot air balloon with logo," "meteorologist in a computer lab," and the bizarre one: "Levitate an actual cloud." Ridiculous? Absolutely. But it sparked a conversation about skywriting and weather balloons.

LOOK for Sparks

Congratulations , you've painted the walls with ideas in rainbow marker. Now grab a flamethrower, metaphorically speaking, and ignite those sparks. Literally sift through your doodle jungle like you're prospecting for gold. Some ideas will roar out like fireworks; others will need a match.

FIRST, step back and stare. Do some ideas glue themselves together? Maybe three different folks scribbled "floating," "levitate," and "anti-gravity" in different corners. Aha! That cluster screams "meteorology meets MTV." Circle it, highlighter it, tattoo it. These patterns are your coals that just need puffing.

. . .

PLAY CURATOR: set aside anything that even made one person's eyes light up. Even the weird ones. Then mix and match. Could two half-ideas fuse into something cooler? In one brainstorm, we found ourselves with two orphan ideas: "interactive inflatable cloud" and "dance." Next thing we knew, the "Cloud Dance Lounge" was born , a thousand-pound inflated cloud block with a DJ booth inside. (There are no bad ideas in brainstorming.)

ANOTHER TRICK: have folks act out or explain the wild ones. "Picture this!" I once said when someone mentioned a 'fashion belt show'. Suddenly we had our very own mini-runway show demonstration in the meeting. By physically reenacting, the team spotted potential we missed on paper: maybe we shouldn't belt-punchout, but a wearable billboard belt for model dog-walkers? It started there.

WE'VE ALSO GOT **the old "What if?" game**. Take a semi-interesting idea and ask "What if we did that but.. reversed? Or in a garage sale? Or on Mars?" The goal is to generate secondary sparks from initial sparks. For example, an idea about a "cloud piñata" turned into "what if we did a piñata pinata of a cloud on a bus during SXSW?" You'd think that's barking mad, but "Branded bus at SXSW with cloud piñatas" got people's attention , and free marshmallows in their mouths.

ENCOURAGE FRIENDLY DEBATE: invite a naysayer to challenge an idea, because resistance often unearths new directions. If someone balks at "cloud club" being absurd, press them: "Okay genius, how would that work?" Their answer might actually refine it into something doable. We once had to explain a levitating cloud stunt to a client, and their "That's impossible" challenge forced us to think of digital projection instead. The outcome wasn't flying a cloud over Times Square, but something just as magical: holograms on water mist.

And don't forget: Weirdness is gold. If an idea looks like something your teenage cousin's fever dream might cook up, give it the spotlight. Fancy-word business proposals suck the life out of creativity. Instead, say it like it is: "A cloud-disco called The Cumulous Club." Or, "Let's dress everyone up in 70s gangster outfits and have them deliver the password to the afterparty like a secret handshake." If you're laughing or cringing, you're on the right track. Safety is overrated when you need sparks.

EXPAND, Twist, Reframe

Got a spark? Great. Now fan it into a wildfire. Take that half-baked kernel and twist it into something even crazier. If it's an idea about a cloud, ask "How many more layers can we add? How can we make this 10x bolder?" You want something share-worthy, not boring.

Think of this step like sculpting a snowball into a toboggan of epic proportions. You can stretch it: if the idea was a single runway belt show, could it be a flash mob where everyone's pants literally fall down into a pair of branded shorts with giant belt-buckles? If one bus isn't enough, why not a whole fleet playing a synchronized jazz band moving through the streets? The goal is to disrupt comfort zones.

CASE IN POINT: that bus at SXSW. The initial brain dump included "ads on buses" and "mobile billboard." Meh. But then we dared ourselves: **"What might be all the ways we can be the very first brand impression at this noisy conference"**, "What are all the ways a bus isn't just a bus, but the experience?" Suddenly the plan became: grab people in the baggage area and offer them a lift to their hotel. Save them money and we even hired improv actors to chat up the people in their seats to entertain and sell our product.

ANOTHER EXAMPLE: We had an idea about levitating clouds. Sounds insane? Good. Instead of backing off, ask how to make it plausible or how to spin it. Maybe we literally can't levitate a cloud, but what if we make a cloud-simulating drone swarm that spells out a hashtag over the city? Boom, from fantasy to a guerrilla skywriting campaign that became the talk of Twitter. Or we thought of a "cloud pillow fort" inside a mall: by stacking cotton and lights to make shoppers think they were stepping into an actual cloud. All of these expanded the original weirdness into something shareable.

The same goes for small ideas: maybe someone says "light bulbs" randomly. Don't dismiss it: maybe light bulbs can signify "bright ideas," so you turn the entire brainstorming room into a lamp factory-themed mad lab. Or "light bulbs that float with helium in a lobby." Ridiculous? Perhaps. But when folks leave scratching their heads, you know it worked. We once had light bulbs suspended by drones at an event , an illumination installation we dubbed "Idea Air." Wild? Sure. But memorable? You bet.

KEEP REFRAMING. If one angle isn't juicy enough, ask "What if we went opposite? If 'cloud' was warm and fluffy, what if we go gritty and use the idea of a storm instead? If 'fashion belt show' screams runway, what if we threw a belt bungee jump where models freefall?" Even a subtle flip might spark brilliance.

FINALLY, don't let logistics get in the way of imagination. In WoMBAT sessions, "bad idea" is an oxymoron; it's either a stepping stone or a laugh generator. If someone throws in "spray the mayor with whipped cream via catapult," don't snipe it with "No way." Instead, cough politely, lean in, and ask, "Ok, how's the catapult made from recycled credit cards?" Suddenly your brain is doing backflips, and who knows, maybe you're onto a hilarious prototype stunt that ends up on the news.

THE WOMBAT MINDSET: Practice Makes Perfect

By now, your whiteboards look like a kindergarten art warzone, and that's exactly the point. WoMBAT isn't a one-and-done trick , it's a habit, a muscle. The more you muscle through these steps, the sharper your brain's imagination gets. Think of creativity like a pickup truck: it runs better with good oil changes, not if you just bought it and never used it. If you only do a WoMBAT session once in a blue moon, you'll be rusty. But do it over and over, and soon the first truly wild-card idea pops up in your head every time the question "What might be all the ways…" slides out of your mouth.

YOU'LL ALSO LEARN this truth fast: The best ideas usually come late in the marathon, not at the starting gun. Don't bail after ten minutes because "nothing good is happening." Keep going. Dig deeper. The first wave was just the warm-up. Some of my greatest successes came after people were exhausted, leaning on each other for support, about to give up , and then something struck like lightning.

SO KEEP PRACTICING these steps with every problem, big or small. Next time your work buddy complains about writer's block, suggest a mini-WoMBAT. Next brainstorm, be the one who shouts, "Clouds, cats, cookies , what are all the ways to use anything to solve this?" You'll surprise yourself with the spaghetti junction of creativity that follows.

AND WHEN IN DOUBT, remember: Nobody ever stood up at a party and said, "Man, I'm so glad we opted for the safe, paper-napkin idea on that campaign." They'll remember the belt models, the floating clouds, the party bus , because those move the needle. Those get talked about at water coolers, not snooze-fests.

· · ·

SO STOP SETTLING FOR "MEH" ideas that could be invented by literally any committee. You've got permission (no, an obligation) to be bold, a little crazy, and a lot original. Your brand is begging for it , and the market has zero patience for vanilla. If WoMBAT teaches us anything, it's this: Your brain is capable of outrageous creativity, but it needs a nudge. Give it that nudge again and again, and watch it do a backflip.

NOW GO FORTH and WoMBAT like a boss. Your next great idea is out there , maybe half-baked in someone's dusty mind. It's up to you to tease it out, amplify it, and throw it a parade. After all, would you rather be remembered for safe squares or swinging for the creative fences? (Spoiler: safe squares never win.) So charge those dice, toss aside that napkin, and start asking the only question that matters: What might be ALL the ways we can blow people's minds today?

GET WEIRD OR GO HOME: Why Your Brain Needs Odd Fuel

Ever sit in a marketing meeting hearing the same tired buzzwords and wonder why your brain hasn't exploded yet? That's because everything you're consuming is stale industry fodder. If all you feed your brain is the same trends and copycat ideas, the output will be as bland as decaf coffee. Great creative ideas need something far spicier, freakish, diverse inputs, not another LinkedIn carousel.

BEWARE the Echo Chamber

For example, tabloids once spun a bizarre story that Yankees legend Derek Jeter sent one-night stands home with autographed gift baskets. People ate it up. Jeter finally laughed it off, asking incredulously "who would believe that nonsense? And you believed it!". If a rumor that weird can trend, imagine what you could do by leaning into the odd on purpose.

Even more extreme: GoldenPalace.com (an online casino) once spent $28,000 on a Virgin Mary grilled cheese and $65,000 on a haunted cane , not to eat or use them, but for pure marketing shock. "We're not crazy," shrugged their marketer, "we're just glad you're talking about it". Sure enough, outlets from The Washington Post to Time to the BBC covered the story. Even McDonald's spoofed the stunt in a Super Bowl ad. All told, roughly $1M spent got press worth many millions. Related but kinda not. I stole that Virgin Mary idea to launch a startup but I am going to save that story for a podcast or something.

THE DIVERSITY DIVIDEND

It's not just anecdotes , research proves this. Culturally diverse teams deliver better outcomes because they bring a wider range of perspectives and information to the table. McKinsey found diverse teams outperform homogeneous ones by 36% in profitability. Boston Consulting Group reports companies with diverse leadership earn 19% more of their revenue from innovation. When different brains collide, they create sparks nobody saw coming.

And what about that squishy universe between your ears? It turns out boring your brain can actually spark genius. Psychologists call boredom a "variety-seeking emotion" that primes you to seek fresh experiences and solutions. In one study, people forced to do a tedious task later produced more creative ideas afterward , their minds had been hunting for novelty. Even author David Burkus noted that after a 10-hour sales meeting, the breakthroughs only came during the after-dinner drinks.

. . .

FEAST Your Eyes on the New and Weird

So what are these "strange inputs"? Pop-culture mashups, oddball history or just plain weird stuff. Think of Steve Jobs studying Zen gardens and calligraphy so Macs could have beautiful fonts, or Tarantino devouring samurai films and spaghetti westerns to remake Hollywood. If you only copy other marketing campaigns, your output will never pop.

Instead, binge content outside your bubble. Read an indie sci-fi novel; watch a foreign prank show; flip through a kids' comic from the 1970s. Have coffee with someone who builds custom arcade cabinets or mixes creative cocktails , they'll think differently. Photocopy a page from an obscure magazine or jot down a cool font you spot on a coffee cup. All those weird references become your toolkit. The more you know about random corners of culture, the more Lego bricks your brain has to build with.

ACTIONABLE TACTICS to Collect and Remix Inspiration

Subscribe to the Weird: Force-feed yourself randomness. Follow newsletters or feeds that have nothing to do with your industry , astrophysics, avant-garde art, retro video games, you name it. Set Google Alerts for ridiculous phrases. (Alert for "flamingo skateboarding incident," anyone?) Your inbox will overflow with "WTF?" content that jolts your brain awake.

HOARD THE ODDBALLS: Keep an Idea Fridge , a digital folder or Slack channel where you dump inspiring oddities: wild news clips, bizarre ads, vintage flyers, memes you can't unsee. When ideation stalls, raid the fridge. (Even a stock photo of a lemur eating spaghetti might spark "Monty Python meets Client X.") Revisit and riff on these gems regularly, not just in crunch time.

SCHEDULE BOREDOM BREAKS: Pencil in idle moments. No screens, no agendas, just you and a daydream. Try silent walks, long showers, or the classic "flush-and-think." Think of these as gym time for your mind. Studies show letting your mind wander often unlocks unexpected creativity. (Yes, that 15-minute "nothing" break could be your best strategy yet.)

CROSS-POLLINATE: Talk to people outside your silo. Grab lunch with a software dev, a grocery clerk, or a philosophy major. Ask them to explain something they love. Their fresh perspectives are like exotic spices in your idea stew. I ask all new hires to read 2 specific books (now three I guess) and even starts some projects by making everyone watch a movie (I loves Pee-wee's Big Adventure or Beauty is Embarrassing for this) to prime the team with unusual vibes.

TRAVEL (BRAIN-TRAVEL): Literally or mentally, venture somewhere new. Visit a museum, a subculture club, or just a different neighborhood. Explore a science museum or an international market. Snap photos of interesting typography or architecture, or curate a playlist of foreign pop songs. New places and faces reset your brain's assumptions and fuel fresh ideas.

GREAT CREATIVITY ISN'T factory work , it's a scavenger hunt through weirdness. If you keep sipping the same safe milkshake of trade shows and branded content, your brain will barf out a bland smoothie. Mix in the absurd: that odd YouTube saga, that crazy restaurant logo, or that viral meme with a Pomeranian in a suit. The richer the input buffet, the more mouthwatering your ideas become. Get weird. Your ideas (and everyone else's) will thank you.

6 /
wombat - the list

WHEN I FIRST STARTED THINKING ABOUT this book, I'll be real with you , it was 90% ego, 10% good intentions. My original plan was to create the ultimate bathroom reader: a thick, indulgent stack of pages, each one spotlighting a different stunt or idea I'd pulled off over the years. A vanity project in the truest sense. Five or six pages per caper. Lots of "look what I did!" energy.

There's some value in that kind of thing. But eventually, I realized teaching the method behind the madness , the why and how of the ideas , was going to be more useful. Still, there's a loud, obnoxious voice in my brain that keeps screaming, "SHOW THEM THE FUN STUFF!" So this chapter is that voice getting its way.

IT'S NOT the whole book , but it's the victory lap portion. A not-so-rapid-fire list of stunts, ideas, and beautifully weird executions. Some made headlines. Some should have. Some got me dragged into meetings I wasn't invited to. All of them made people talk.

This is my story museum. Wander freely. Touch everything.

• • •

INTERNET ALL-STAR BASEBALL Cards

Here's the thing: when you're going to a giant conference and trying to make a splash, you've got two options , show up like everyone else, or blow the doors off.

Everyone dumps the usual swag into the conference tote bag , stickers, t-shirts, maybe a branded pen if they're feeling generous. We wanted to do something nobody had seen before. Something people would remember and talk about. So we made baseball cards.

Actual, retro-inspired, wax-pack-style Internet All-Star Baseball Cards.

We created a set of 20 or 21 (I can't remember , sue me) cards featuring real FreshBooks users. Three were semi-famous: Tina Roth Eisenberg, Chris Brogan (yes, again), and an early-era Gary Vaynerchuk , back when he was still human-sized and not yet a motivational meme with sneakers. The rest? Just awesome FreshBooks customers. Designers, marketers, developers , everyday folks doing killer work.

EACH CARD LOOKED like a 1980's Topps throwback , fake woodgrain border, a big heroic photo on the front, and the back packed with stats: what the person did, what made them great, how to contact them, and why you should hire them. The FreshBooks logo was there, but small. Because this wasn't about us , it was about making our customers into heroes.

Everyone who had a card in the set got a giant stack of extras to hand out like business cards. We also gave out booster packs at the booth. People started trading them like actual baseball cards. I saw folks hunting down specific ones on the show floor. It created a game, a buzz, a community.

And that was the point. When 20 employees walk around

saying, "Our brand is amazing," it sounds like marketing. But when 100 conference-goers say it without being paid, that's word of mouth. That's WoMBAT.

SOME PEOPLE even completed the entire set. People still talk about them. You can still find pictures of the cards online. It was bold, different, and sticky. And it worked.

Killing the Mascot

Alright, this one is… complicated. And stupid. And brilliant. And still one of my favorite ideas of all time.

IT NEVER GOT MADE, not because it wasn't good (it was!) , but because no one else was brave enough to say yes. That happens sometimes. You swing big, and people blink.

So here's how it went down.

One day, the CEO at FreshBooks says to me, "We want to kill the mascot." Now, this wasn't a real mascot in a foam suit. It was a cartoon dude named Ivan, a character we used in ads, emails, banners. He was supposed to represent our ideal user. Ivan had been around forever and, like a lot of long-running characters, had gone stale.

The CEO just meant "retire the mascot." Do a little rebrand. Something tasteful.

But that's not how I operate.

Instead, I asked myself the only question that matters: What are all the ways we could kill a mascot? Like, really kill him.

So I came up with this campaign. Ivan, the lovable everyman face of FreshBooks, would contract a fictional terminal illness. Not right away , we'd play the long game. Slowly, over the course of six months, he'd appear in marketing materials looking thinner... weaker... then he'd show up in an IV drip... then one day, boom , he's slumped over in a chair. Gone.

WE'D CAP it off with a fake obituary and a press release: "Ivan has passed. In lieu of flowers, please donate to the Free-lancers Union." Tastefully dark. Satirical. Emotional. Weirdly moving.

It would've been epic.

But no one else thought so.

TO BE FAIR, this was pre-WoMBAT Saul. But it was pure WoMBAT thinking: "What are all the ways we can turn something small into something loud, funny, and shareable?" A boring brand refresh? Nah. A fictional death? Now we're talking.

Ultimately, the idea didn't pass the sniff test. Too weird. Too morbid. Too... everything. But it's stayed with me for over a decade because I still think it had legs.

· · ·

AND FUNNY ENOUGH, other brands have since killed their mascots. Sometimes literally , falling off cliffs, disappearing in sad goodbye posts , but never with this level of satire or heart. No charity angle. No arc. No buildup.

Just lazy executions without the bite. Mine? Mine had bite and soul.

Sure, it never happened. But I still think about Ivan. RIP, buddy. You would've died beautifully.

THE ARMORED TRUCK

Here's a fun truth that sounds made up but isn't: even in the era of Venmo and blockchain and instant wire transfers, a lot of small businesses still run on paper checks.

So when there's a postal strike , which, yeah, still happens , it doesn't just inconvenience people. It screws with their cash flow. It messes with their ability to survive.

And survival is the whole game.

One year, during one of those inevitable mail strikes, I asked myself (again): What are all the ways we could help our customers? What are all the ways we can show we actually give a shit? What are all the ways we can do something good... and maybe get a little attention while we're at it?

The answer?

We rented an armored truck. A full-on, Brinks-style, bulletproof, "this truck might have the nuclear codes" kind of truck.

And I drove it.

Seriously. I drove the truck , with a my work buddy Sarah Wibore riding shotgun , around the city picking up physical checks from FreshBooks customers and delivering them, by hand, to where they needed to go.

Not because it scaled. Not because it was efficient. Because it was the right kind of crazy.

Because it said, loud and clear: we're in this with you.

And sure, it made the local news. It made the blogs. We got some fun media hits out of it. But the thing that mattered most? The trust it built. The stories those small businesses told afterward.

It's easy to send a tweet saying "we support small business." It's another thing to rent an 8-ton bank vault on wheels and use it to play financial Santa Claus during a goddamn postal breakdown.

It wasn't about branding. It was about loyalty. About doing good.

Also? Driving that beast was awesome.

7TH BIRTHDAY PARTY

Milestones matter. Not in a "we hit our KPIs" kind of way , I'm talking about real milestones. Ones that deserve balloons, confetti, and at least one person dressed as a magician who may or may not have insurance.

So when FreshBooks turned seven, I didn't want to just send an internal Slack emoji or update the footer on the website. I wanted a party. Not just any party , a full-blown, seven-year-old's birthday party. But for adults. At a professional conference.

WHY?

BECAUSE NO ONE remembers the booth with the retractable banner and free pens. But they will remember the one with balloon animals, clowns, fire eaters, ice cream sandwich makers, and a carnival-style atmosphere that made everyone wonder if they accidentally microdosed before walking into the event hall.

We had it all , a photo booth, rides, a live magician, and

even an ice cream sandwich eating contest. Not kidding. I still remember the look on one attendee's face when they realized they were on CNN because of a dessert competition. That's peak conference ROI.

This wasn't just about fun. It was strategy in face paint. We asked ourselves, "What are all the ways we can make people feel something about our brand?" What are all the ways we can surprise them, delight them, and get them to drop their guards and say, "Okay... tell me more."

The party got people talking. It got us on national news. It got thousands of ice cream sandwiches into the hands of hungry, confused, delighted attendees. And it got FreshBooks remembered , not for accounting software, but for giving people something worth remembering.

If your brand turns seven and you don't throw a birthday party with a balloon artist and a fire breather, are you even trying?

TIMES SQUARE BILLBOARD

Sometimes thinking differently isn't about reinventing the wheel. Sometimes it's about noticing something that everyone else is ignoring , and jumping on it before the window closes.

Now, I'll admit: this idea wasn't life-changing. It didn't revolutionize a brand. But it's one of my favorite small bets with a big return , and it all started with me sitting in the middle of Times Square, wondering how the hell someone gets on one of those giant digital billboards.

IF YOU'VE NEVER BEEN, Times Square is this electric, chaotic, sensory overload of a place where it's somehow just as bright at 2 a.m. as it is at 2 p.m. , a never-ending circus that's both thrilling and deeply weird. It's like Las Vegas and your iPhone home screen had a baby that only knows how to scream in brand voice.

ANYWAY, I was there one day, looking up at the American Eagle store, and I noticed something strange. Their massive digital wall , which stretches up the side of the building , was showcasing photo after photo of sad-looking people. Not dramatic, just... miserable shoppers with thousand-yard stares. And I couldn't figure out why.

So I walked into the store and asked an employee: "Why does your billboard look like a funeral slideshow?"

Turns out, at that time, if you bought anything at American Eagle, even a keychain, they'll take your picture and put you on the billboard. It's their in-store experience. You buy, you pose, you go up.

So I did what anyone who believes in seizing an opportunity would do: I sprinted back to my hotel, grabbed a sweatshirt with the logo of the startup I was representing at the time, ran back, bought the cheapest thing they had (that $2 keychain), and got my photo taken.

The next part was key: there was a 20-minute delay between taking the photo and having it go live on the billboard. So I spent that time setting up cameras, doing man-on-the-street interviews, and asking strangers, "Hey, do you know who that is on the billboard?"

Spoiler alert: they didn't. But the footage was gold.

THE RESULT? A piece of content that looked like we had bought our way onto one of the most iconic advertising stages in the world... for two bucks.

The startup got over a million impressions from that one stunt. And to this day, people still think we actually bought the billboard space.

That's the thing. Marketing isn't always about blowing the budget , sometimes it's about seeing the angle, thinking quickly, and turning a goofy loophole into something unforgettable.

AND YES, I still have the keychain.

Cigar Climbing Stunt

So this idea probably could get its own chapter if not its own book this one falls under the category of you know the one that got away or the the greatest idea I've ever had that didn't get executed The "drop the mic, blow up the internet, get sued just enough to make it exciting" kind of idea. And yet… it never happened. Not because we didn't try. Oh, we tried , like planning-a-heist levels of try. But we'll get to that.

SO A LUXURY CIGAR STARTUP , think rare, $3,000-a-stick kind of stuff , came to me and said the magic words: "We just got funded and want the craziest idea you can dream up."

Now, normally when a brand says that, they don't mean it. They want edgy-but-safe. They want "Wow" with a clear ROI. They say "crazy" but they mean "quaintly quirky with an explainer video."

But these folks? They meant it. I pitched them several solid, brand-aligned ideas , smart, newsworthy, attention-grabbing. And they kept saying: "Crazier." Then they said: "Forget the brand. We just want the most ridiculous thing possible. We want to be on TV."

SO NOW I'M in dangerous territory. This isn't my usual kind of brief, because I like ideas that tie back to something. Revenue, community, loyalty , purpose. But they didn't care. They wanted stunts for the sake of stunts. And I'm not gonna lie, I can do that… but I do it with some hesitation. Not because I can't pull it off , I can , but because I hate wasting a good idea on nothing.

Still, I gave them what they asked for.

ENTER: French Spiderman

BACK WHEN I WAS A KID, I used to watch this guy on Wide World of Sports , a real daredevil. No harness, no gear, just chalked hands and a death wish, scaling skyscrapers with nothing but finger strength and misplaced confidence. He'd climb stuff like the CN Tower or the World Trade Center (pre-9/11), get arrested, and make the evening news. It was pure spectacle.

So I said: let's hire that guy to climb a glass skyscraper in Los Angeles. About three-quarters of the way up, he'd hit a trigger on a special custom-built backpack, which would deploy a massive telescoping banner , like a giant car dealership flag , with the cigar company's logo and URL. Then he'd finish the climb, get arrested (as expected), and boom: global press.

AND I DON'T MEAN this was just a pitch deck. We planned everything. I tracked the climber down , which required a bit of digital detective work , and sent him the idea. He loved it. His exact reply?

Hi Saul.

Let's try today although at this hour I'm still in custody in Philippines.
Best regards
Alain ps should be out today

I still consider that the greatest email I've ever received.

WE FOUND the perfect building in LA, booked hotel rooms across the street on four different floors to film from multiple hights and angles, hired a drone crew, commissioned a Hollywood prop shop to build the backpack and the spring-loaded flagpole... we even budgeted for legal fees in case we got arrested. Which we absolutely would have.

• • •

HELL, we even planned to call the police on ourselves , anonymously , so traffic choppers would catch the stunt live and it would make the local news and end up on police logs. We hired extras to hang around the sidewalk and point at the sky like a flash mob of astonished looky-loos. Every single detail was planned.

And then… one week before go-time, the client pulled the plug.

Why? Because (and this part kills me), they said:

"It doesn't really tie back to our brand goals."

The exact thing I had warned them about. The same thing they told me not to worry about. But hey, that's showbiz.

We got paid a tiny chunk for our time , not what we deserved, but enough to sleep at night , and all the vendors got taken care of. But to this day, this is the one that got away.

WOULD IT HAVE GONE VIRAL? Absolutely.

Would it have sparked legal issues? Also yes.

Would it have been unforgettable? Without question.

IT WAS BOLD, bonkers, and meticulously planned. Just not the right bold bonkers. I still think about that backpack.

One project we did execute for this brand was we made "parking signs" and put them all over the city at the time of the Pebble Beach Car show. One of the largest HNW car get together and auctions. because the city is small and the event pushes the capacity to the limit parking is at a premium and we blocked off the whole city and people thought they had to join the community to park anywhere...and yes we did this without permission of the city and it was a huge success.

WHOOSH!

Whoosh! is one of those brands that makes you want to hug your client contact and say, "Thank you for not being boring." Canadian-founded, gutsy, and deeply aware that a sense of humor is a competitive advantage, Whoosh! wasn't just a fun brand to work with , it was a fun brand that let us go full throttle. And honestly? That's rarer than it should be.

Now, if you don't know Whoosh!, here's the gist: it's a spray that disinfects your phone screen. Think Purell, but for the germy slab you press to your face 40 times a day. Their whole thing is that your phone is gross , and they're absolutely right. It is. And most people don't realize that their phone is 10x dirtier than a public toilet seat.

So we weaponized that fact.

We started with good old-fashioned man-on-the-street videos. Walk up to strangers, test their phones for bacteria, show them the results (which were always horrific), clean the screen with Whoosh!, and then test it again. Cue shocked faces, nervous laughs, dramatic gasps. Basically, we captured human disgust and turned it into a brand asset. These videos worked because they were real. People felt them. You could practically smell the germs through your screen.

WHOOSH! Man on the Street Test #WhylWhoosh - Saul Colt The Idea Integration Company
6,153 views

But the pièce de résistance , the campaigns that still make me giggle , were the ones we ran at CES, the giant consumer electronics trade show in Vegas. CES is a loud, flashy circus. Everyone's yelling. Everyone's trying to be the most "cutting edge." So how do you stand out? You do the opposite. You make things stupidly simple and stupidly human.

WE DESIGNED their entire trade show booth around the old-school comic strip Family Circus. You remember those dotted-line maps that showed Billy running all over the damn house, out the window, into the yard, under the couch, and back again? We recreated that. Giant installation, dotted lines and all , tracking where your phone goes in a day. Subways, public washrooms, gym floors, café tables, and so on. Each stop on the route made your phone more disgusting, and at the end of the path was , wait for it , a Whoosh! cleaning station. It was whimsical, nostalgic, and totally on-brand. And it made people stop, smile, and clean their phones.

But the real slam dunk? The bathroom stickers.

THIS IS one of my favorite stunts of all time. We designed a set of 11x17 stickers made to look like text message conversations , funny, smart, and gross in all the right ways. The exchange went something like:

PERSON 1: "I'm texting you from the toilet."

Person 2: "Congrats , that toilet is 10x cleaner than your phone."

CTA: "Come to booth #xxxx and get your phone cleaned."
And then... we went rogue.

. . .

WITHOUT ASKING permission (a recurring theme you'll notice in my work), we hired a small crew of college kids and blanketed the back of every single stall in the entire conference center. We're talking close to 900 stalls across multiple buildings. That means anyone who sat down , to do their business or just hide from networking , looked up and saw a message that said, in so many words: Your phone is filthier than the bowl you're sitting on.

It was attention-grabbing. It was gross. It was hilarious. And most importantly, it worked.

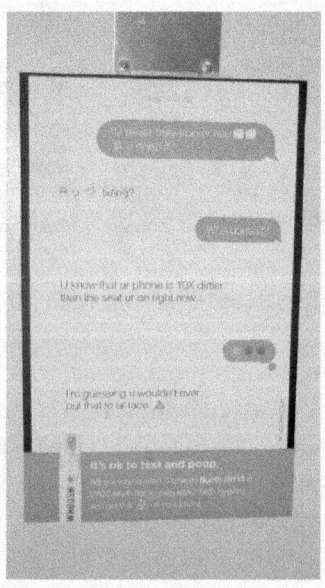

Between the Family Circus booth, the toilet stickers, and the videos, Whoosh! had their best CES ever , by a long shot. I'm not at liberty to say exactly how much product moved, but let's just say it was more than double their previous best and the foot traffic was so high they had to reprint collateral on the second day. That's the power of asking, "What are all the ways…"

WAS IT BOLD? Yep.

Did we break a few rules? Sure.
Did people remember the brand? Hell yes, they did.
And that's the goal, isn't it?

HOW TO WRITE for TV

This is one of those stories where the idea sneaks up on you disguised as something else , in this case, as a podcast episode , and ends up being one of the best things we did for building a new vertical at Xero. But let's rewind.

I'VE GOT this friend named David Feldman. If you don't know him, that's fine , he does a lot of his best work in the background. But trust me when I say he's one of the best comedy writers working today. This guy has written for Steve Martin, Martin Short, Jeff Ross, The Daily Show, Bill Maher, and basically every Comedy Central Roast that's ever made someone cry backstage. The man has chops.

DAVID ALSO HAD A PODCAST , it's still around, but these days it's drifted more toward politics, which is his thing. Back then, though? It was a goldmine of comedy nerd content. Sketches, interviews, deep-dive conversations with writers and comics, and just general brilliance wrapped in self-deprecation. So when I was at Xero , which, as you probably know, is accounting software for small businesses , I saw a bit of an open lane.

. . .

HERE'S THE CONTEXT: we wanted to get more creative professionals using Xero. Designers, writers, filmmakers, comedians , the types of people who were probably tracking their expenses in a pizza-stained notebook or not at all. And we figured, instead of trying to sell to them directly, what if we gave them something valuable first? Something that spoke to their dreams, not just their tax deductions.

SO I STARTED ASKING: What are all the ways we can connect with creatives? What are all the ways we can show we get them? What are all the ways we can give them something they'll actually care about... that just happens to have our logo in the corner?

ENTER: How to Write for Television , a two-hour masterclass disguised as a podcast episode.

We partnered with David, who pulled in a murderer's row of TV writers from shows like Seinfeld, Arrested Development, The Daily Show, and more. These weren't washed-up "used to be on CBS" types , these were active, working pros. And they brought it. They shared war stories. Talked about breaking into the industry. Dropped real, tactical advice. They even got vulnerable about the stuff they wish they knew before their first writer's room meltdown.

And through it all, Xero was subtly, proudly present. Not intrusive. Not cheesy. Just a gentle nudge that this was the kind of brand that got you.

WE PROMOTED IT HARD. Shared it across David's network. Pushed it to every guest's audience. Dropped it in creative Facebook groups, Reddit threads, and design school email blasts. And you know what? It worked.

Almost. One. Million. Downloads.

Let me say that again: Almost One million. For an accounting brand podcast episode that didn't have a single quick tip about reconciling your bank statement.

It became a calling card. People still reference it online. It gave us real traction with a completely new audience that probably wouldn't have touched Xero otherwise. And it proved something

I'VE ALWAYS BELIEVED:

Give people something worth sharing, and they'll do the work for you.

No gimmicks. No hacks. Just value. Wrapped in smart creative. Driven by a single question: What are all the ways…

SMALL BUSINESS ACCOUNTING Day at the State Capitol

(aka That Time I Almost Got Deported for a Sandwich)

You ever wonder who decides there's a "National Cookie Day" or "Hug Your Cat Day" or whatever other nonsense fills up your calendar and your inbox with limited-time offers on oat milk? I did. And when I looked into it, I realized… there's no official registry. You can literally just declare something a national day and run with it.

SO, we did.

WHILE I WAS AT XERO, we were always looking for ways to get deeper into the small business community , to not just serve them but stand with them. To say, "We see you. We're with you. We'll show up." That's what led to the invention of Small Business Accounting Day at the California State Capitol.

And no, we didn't ask for permission. Because the truth is: if you're waiting for someone to give you a day, you'll be waiting a long time. We made our own.

We brought 50 small business owners and 20 small-business-focused CPAs to Sacramento, threw up a tent on the front lawn of the Capitol building, and created an all-out carnival. Not a metaphorical carnival , we had actual food trucks, picnic tables, branded everything, and a vibe that said, "This is not your average lobbying event."

The point was simple: get the folks inside the building , the people who make policy, vote on laws, and rarely, if ever, talk to the real humans their decisions affect , to come outside, grab a sandwich, and listen.

Now, was this a little manipulative? Yeah. Did we use a bit of guilt? Absolutely. But here's the deal , it worked. A ton of actual legislators came out. They shook hands. They heard real stories. They understood pain points that no lobbying email ever conveyed. And those small business owners felt seen.

We filmed everything. Captured testimonials. Used it as content for months.

But here's the kicker , and the part that gets the most laughs when I tell this story on stage:

I got detained inside the Capitol.

YEP. Full-on taken aside by security. Not arrested, not cuffed, but definitely not free to leave. Apparently when you set up an unauthorized branded event on government property , even one that gives away sandwiches and love , someone's going to ask questions.

They held me for an hour. Wanted to know who I was, why I was there, and who the hell gave me the authority to declare a new holiday on the Capitol lawn.

I played the Canadian card real hard. I apologized 400 times. Promised we were just packing up and leaving , which, by the way, was always the plan. We only intended to stay through lunch. The state felt like they had shut us down. We felt like we got everything we came for. Win-win.

No one got arrested. The footage was amazing. And best of all? The message landed.

Because this is WoMBAT at work:

What are all the ways we can show our customers we care?

What are all the ways we can make them feel important?

What are all the ways we can actually help them , beyond the software, beyond the ads?

SOMETIMES, the best marketing move is a sandwich and a smile… and the guts to risk getting kicked out of a government building.

VOITURES Extravert

(Or, The Time We Marketed the Prettiest Car You've Never Driven)

Let's start with this: I love Porsche. Specifically, I dream of owning a 911. I have since I was a kid. It's the kind of car that lives in your soul rent-free, even if it never actually makes it into your driveway. So, when I heard about a company in the Netherlands turning classic 1970s and '80s Porsche 911s into electric vehicles , not just slapping a Tesla battery in and calling it a day, but actually reengineering them with love, precision, and proprietary tech , I became obsessed. And I do not use that word lightly.

· · ·

THAT COMPANY WAS VOITURES EXTRAVERT. From the moment I saw their cars, I knew we had to work with them. And by we, I mean The Idea Integration Co., my agency , the place where we turn "what ifs" into headlines.

Now, this wasn't a giant funded startup with VC money to burn and "move fast" tattooed on their decks. It was a true indie brand: engineering brilliance, artisanal spirit, but not a lot of gas in the marketing tank. No splashy budget. No Super Bowl ad dreams. No giant American footprint. Our job? Fix all of that , on a shoestring.

AND READER, we fucking did.

THE CHALLENGE

They had no North American presence. No cars here. No showroom. Just some very beautiful photos and a handful of European press mentions. The product was real , incredibly real , but from a buyer's perspective, it might as well have been a concept car.

And here's the kicker: these weren't casual Sunday cruisers. Each car started at $400,000 USD.

They were bespoke masterpieces. Not something you "add to cart" after your morning espresso. Our audience wasn't car enthusiasts; it was high-net-worth individuals with an eye for taste, design, and exclusivity , and a deep aversion to risk. So, how do you sell something no one's ever touched, sat in, or driven... especially something that costs more than most condos?

Enter WoMBAT.

STEP ONE: Skip the Funnel

No ads. No drip campaigns. No SEO. None of the stuff that feels "safe" but burns budget while delivering nothing but "awareness." That doesn't cut it when the price tag hits half a million and the stakes are "legacy," not "lead gen."

INSTEAD, we went direct to the people who already had the trust of our audience. We asked ourselves: What are all the ways we can make this car famous without ever placing it in a dealership?

AND THAT'S when the referral flywheel started to spin.

THE PLAYBOOK: Referral Royalty

We built two very specific, very strategic lists:

LUXURY REAL ESTATE AGENTS , specifically those who had sold over $1 billion in residential real estate in the last calendar year. These are the gatekeepers of the ultra-wealthy, the people who know exactly who's buying homes that come with garages fit for art pieces on wheels.

Film Industry Agents and Producers , especially those repping Tier 1 talent. These folks know the elite, influence the aspirational, and understand the value of a flex that's more rare than a Rolex and cooler than a Bugatti.

We offered a $25,000 referral fee for every successful sale. No fine print. No expiry. If you got us a buyer, we cut you a check. Or if you wanted the car, you got $25K off. It was simple, clean, and unlike anything else in the category.

And guess what? It worked.

THE RESULTS

We started getting meetings with Tom Hanks' people. With agents you've seen on Netflix reality shows. With some of the biggest names in real estate, luxury concierge services, and collector car circles. Not only did the referral fee get their attention , the product closed the deal.

Because this wasn't just some gimmick EV retrofit. These cars had soul. Weight distribution identical to the original 911. Battery packs where the engine used to sit. Retro interiors with modern hardware. Driving one felt like a time warp that cared about the planet.

People started talking. Sharing. Whispering in rooms we'd never even stepped foot in. We created desire before the cars ever touched American soil. That's WoMBAT in a nutshell.

We also developed a visual identity for the U.S. market. Created all the materials. Designed the brand book. Consulted on events, dinner experiences, content rollouts, and influencer outreach. We were the AOR, but more than that, we were the stewards of the North American dream for this company.

THE HEARTBREAK

And then… production stalled. Not because of demand , the cars were sold. Not because of marketing , leads were hot and plentiful. The issue was scale. Supply chain. Logistics.

Stuff that's out of the hands of a marketer, even one as persuasive (read: pushy) as me.

Eventually, the company shuttered. I'm still bummed. Still believe in the product. Still think there's a world where they could return and own an entire niche of the luxury EV market. Hell, I'd fund the comeback tour if I could.

But even though the business didn't survive, the work is still some of the best we've ever done. This wasn't just about selling cars. It was about creating mythology. Turning a car into a calling card. A status symbol for the next generation of legacy-builders.

AND THAT'S why I included it here.

BECAUSE BRAVE MARKETING isn't just about wins. It's about trying something most wouldn't. It's about having the audacity to go direct, think differently, and say, "What are all the ways we can do this without playing by the rules?"

THAT'S what we did for Voitures Extravert. And even if they're gone, I still believe we helped build something that mattered.

Bustin Boards

(Grit, Grind, and Grip Tape in the Greatest City on Earth)

Bustin Boards might not be a household name (unless your household includes a halfpipe and some elbow scabs), but to those who know , really know , it's iconic. Not in the mass-produced, skatepark-mall-brand way. I'm talking real-deal, 20-years-deep, East Coast skate heritage. These guys weren't just making boards. They were making statements. And when they asked us to help rebrand, it wasn't about fixing what was broken , it was about amplifying what made them different.

Most skateboard brands lean into the same vibe: palm trees, pools, California sunshine, Venice Beach vibes. That whole laid-back West Coast mythology. But Bustin? Bustin was built in Brooklyn. In the city. On cracked pavement, dodging cabs, bombing bridges. Their story wasn't "chill." It was hustle. Concrete. Transit. And attitude.

That contrast , that authenticity , is what we zeroed in on.

THE BIG QUESTION:

What are all the ways we can make New York a character in the brand, not just a location?

That became our mantra.

THE WORK

We refreshed their identity , new logo, new brand book, full tone-of-voice overhaul. But more importantly, we reposi-tioned the company not just as a skateboard brand, but as a New York skateboard brand. That distinction matters.

Skateboarding on the East Coast isn't recreational , it's functional. You skate to class. You skate to work. You skate to pick up food. It's a gritty, expressive way to navigate chaos. That nuance led us to lean hard into the city as a co-star. The Brooklyn Bridge? It's not a landmark , it's a ramp. The subway isn't a nuisance , it's background music. Taxis, scaffolding, sidewalk cracks? All part of the terrain.

WE EMBEDDED all of that in the brand's DNA.

The visual language shifted from "endless summer" to "midnight session." We used subway textures, aerial city maps, graffiti, and surveillance-camera angles. Think early Beastie Boys meets Do the Right Thing with grip tape.

A NEW YORK STATE of Grind

During the brand development phase, we kept asking WoMBAT-style questions:

What are all the ways we can speak directly to urban skaters?

What are all the ways we can reframe skate-boarding from rebellion to resilience?

What are all the ways we can position this brand as local first, but global in attitude?

. . .

AND SOMEWHERE IN THERE, we hit on this realization: early skate culture and early hip hop culture were parallel movements. Especially in New York. They both came from the streets. From expression. From making something out of nothing. So we channeled that energy.

Bustin's new voice wasn't "cool" , it was real. It didn't beg to be liked. It just was.

We drew a bit of inspiration from the legendary brand Only NY , a brand that lives and breathes that unapologetic NYC energy. Not a copy, not a clone, but a vibe check. We soaked in the attitude and made sure Bustin came out on the other side feeling like something that could only exist here.

AND THAT'S THE KEY, right?

IN A WORLD full of skate brands trying to be everything to everyone, Bustin stood tall saying:

If you get it, you get it. If you don't , go kick-push somewhere else.

WHY IT WORKED

This wasn't just a visual upgrade or a tone tweak. It was a complete reframing of the brand's soul. We didn't invent something new , we amplified what was already there. We reminded the brand of who it was. And we gave its fans a reason to say, "Yeah, that's my brand."

The best branding work doesn't add noise , it dials up the truth.

That's what we did for Bustin Boards. And it's one of

those projects that still makes me proud because it wasn't about screaming louder , it was about owning a point of view so strong that people couldn't ignore it.

FROSTOP

(The Best Root Beer Nobody's Heard Of – And That's the Whole Joke)

LET me start by saying this: I love root beer. And cream soda. And if I'm being honest, probably birch beer, sarsaparilla, and anything that tastes like it could've been brewed by a kindly old prospector with a handlebar mustache. It's one of my quirks. When I travel, I'm not looking for local wines or hot new restaurants. I'm hunting gas station shelves for weird, regional sodas I've never tasted.

So when I stumbled on Frostop, it felt like striking liquid

gold. I had never heard of it. It was sitting unassumingly in a random corner-store fridge. I cracked the cap. Took a sip. And then had a full-blown "where the hell has this been all my life?" moment.

I BECAME OBSESSED. (YES, there is that word again)

AND LIKE ANY GOOD OBSESSIVE, I did what I always do: I called them up and pitched myself.

"LET ME HELP YOU BE HUGE"

I told them I had to work with them. I practically begged. Said I'd do it for fun, for cheap, for root beer , I didn't care. Because from my research, I learned Frostop isn't just a soda brand... it's a hundred-year-old brand. They've got old-school drive-ins across the U.S., they've been featured in films, they've been around since Prohibition-era corner drugstores, and yet , almost nobody's heard of them.

They had an iconic legacy, a super-specific look, and the kind of regional cult status you can't manufacture. All they were missing was someone to poke the world and say, "Hey. You should be drinking this."

Unfortunately, at the time, they weren't ready. Budget. Timing. Whatever. I respected that. But before I walked away, I gave them one pitch , just one , and it's still one of the best ideas I've ever come up with. It's a perfect storm of satire, absurdity, and brand truth.

THE COMMERCIAL That Never Was (But Should Be)
Picture this:
Two people , a man and a woman , sitting in vintage

folding lawn chairs against a stark white backdrop. It's minimal. Dead quiet. They each take a sip of their icy-cold Frostop root beers.

The man leans back and says,

"WE'RE PROBABLY the only two people in the world who even know this stuff exists."

The woman nods… then slowly pulls out a gun, shoots the man, turns to the camera and says,

"Now I'm the only one."

TAGLINE:

Frostop Root Beer. The Best Root Beer in the World That Nobody Knows About It.

DARK? Yes.

Weird? Obviously.

On brand? Perfectly.

WHY? Because Frostop's biggest problem was their obscurity. So instead of fighting that fact, we turned it into the joke. We made the weakness the hook. We leaned into the mystique and treated the brand like a well-kept secret that was too good to share.

It was funny. It was bold. It would have made people do a double take and say, "Wait, what did I just watch?" And those are the ads that work , the ones that zig when everything else zags.

Now, let me be clear: this wasn't shock for shock's sake. The tone was satirical. The execution was tasteful. It wasn't gory or graphic , it was deadpan humor with a pop-culture wink. The kind of thing that lives online, gets passed around, and gives a brand like Frostop exactly what it needs , attention.

WHY This Still Matters

Frostop was a regional brand. They had leeway. They had character. They had flavor , both literally and creatively. And if they had pulled the trigger (pun absolutely intended) on this spot, I have zero doubt it would've lit up social media, food blogs, Reddit threads, and your weird cousin's group chat.

Great marketing doesn't always need a big budget , it needs a big swing. And this was it.

So yeah, it didn't happen. But it still lives rent-free in my brain, because it's a textbook WoMBAT example:

.   **What are all the ways we can embrace who we are?**
What are all the ways we can flip our weakness into a differentiator?
What are all the ways we can make people care?

IF YOU'VE GOT a brand that's unknown , lean into that. Be the mystery. Be the inside joke. Be the punchline that turns into a product people have to try.

Frostop could've owned that.

#IMAL / I Make A Living

(The Day We Turned Small Business Therapy Into a Marketing Strategy)

Let me set the stage.

FreshBooks was in a weird spot. The business was healthy. Revenues were solid. Customer retention was strong. But somewhere along the way, the brand lost its mojo. Nobody hated FreshBooks , but nobody was talking about it either. No tattoos. No tweets about how it saved their life. No "oh my God, I tell every freelancer I meet to use this" evangelism that once filled their inbox.

THEY WEREN'T DISLIKED. They were... tolerated.

WHICH, in branding, is basically a terminal diagnosis.

The team brought me in to fix that.

They didn't need leads or revenue boosts , they needed affection. They needed to be loved again. And I knew we couldn't brute-force that with emails and banner ads. We needed to dig deeper. So I did what I always do: I started talking to real customers.

WHAT I HEARD (and What They Meant)

Here's what I found:

People still relied on the product. They happily paid for it. They still used it daily. But they didn't feel seen anymore. They felt like FreshBooks had become a utility , not a community.

When the company was smaller, customers said they felt like they were part of something. The brand had a personality. They were invited to events. They got handwritten notes. They felt appreciated.

Now? Radio silence.

That distance, even if unintentional, created a slow emotional drift. The product still worked. But the feeling was gone.

On top of that, a lot of people shared a deeper frustration , one I wasn't expecting. They said there's tons of content out there for starting a business. But once you get past those first 6-12 months , once you've burned through your personal network, once your family stops referring you to people, once the adrenaline wears off , nobody tells you how to keep going.

That's when you need real help. That's when the stakes are highest. And that's when they said they felt most alone.

Boom. That was the insight.

And insight is the match. What comes next is the spark.

"WHAT ARE ALL THE WAYS…?"

I fired up the WoMBAT engine and asked:

What are all the ways we can show up for these people?

What are all the ways we can prove we still give a damn?

What are all the ways we can stop acting like a utility and start acting like a partner again?

The answer was simple: create space for the people who keep the economy running , but rarely get asked how they're doing.

THAT'S where I Make A Living (#IMAL) was born.

Therapy Disguised as a Tour

#IMAL wasn't a roadshow. It was small business group therapy with better lighting.

Each month, Meryl Manning, Francisco Arizmendi, Mike Edge and myself would go to a new city and host an event , part panel, part meetup, part heart-to-heart , where we brought together local small business owners, freelancers, creative entrepreneurs, and anyone brave (or broke) enough to work for themselves.

The format was simple but powerful:

A handpicked panel of four local business owners (some FreshBooks users, some not).

Me as the emcee and moderator, steering the conversation away from the polished Instagram story and into the messy middle.

A real, honest discussion about what's hard, what's work-ing, what's terrifying, and what they wish they'd known sooner.

AND THAT WAS JUST the beginning.

After that, we gave them tools. Talks about where ideas come from. Creative marketing deep dives. Networking, without the awkward "here's my business card" dance. Then we built an online community, so the connection didn't die when the free coffee ran out.

Over time, #IMAL became a tribe. A lifeline.

And here's the kicker: it worked because it wasn't about FreshBooks.

We didn't shove product demos down people's throats. We didn't measure success in trials started. We created genuine value. Emotional value. Strategic value. Human value.

Scale, Then Scale Some More

When we did our first event, I think 18 people showed up.

When I left 18 months later, we were getting 800+ RSVPs per city.

The online community grew like wildfire. Alumni kept in touch. Panelists got business from other attendees. People made lifelong friends. Someone told me after one event that it was "the first time in months I felt like I wasn't doing this alone."

We even turned it into a podcast , a Top 50 Business Podcast on iTunes , so that people who couldn't make it in person could still learn, laugh, and feel a little less lost.

And remember , this whole thing came from asking what are all the ways we can show love to our customers?

NOT SELL TO THEM.

Not trick them.
Not upsell them.

JUST. Show. Love.

Because love is louder than ads. It's louder than churn. And it sure as hell is louder than a banner with a discount code.

WHY THIS MATTERS (A Lot)

#IMAL wasn't just marketing , it was a mission reset.

It reconnected FreshBooks with its core audience, reignited customer passion, and proved (again) that creative, human-centered marketing isn't fluffy or optional. It's effective.

It generated buzz, content, loyalty, and word of mouth , all the good stuff that's impossible to fake and expensive to buy.

It's also a reminder that you don't need to be loud , you just need to be real. Meet people where they are. Listen to them. Show up. Over and over.

And guess what? People talk about that.

THAT'S WORD OF MOUTH. That's WoMBAT. That's the whole damn point.

A NEVER-ENDING QUESTION. A mindset. A tool. A prompt.

And maybe most importantly, a way to stay curious when everyone else is settling.

EVERY STORY YOU JUST READ , from toilet stall guerrilla marketing to $400,000 electric Porsches sold through real estate agents , came from sitting with the question: What are all the ways…?

THAT'S where the best ideas hide. In the cracks between the obvious. WoMBAT is how you go wide. How you surprise yourself. How you find the angles no one else is looking for.

But , and this is key , coming up with ideas isn't enough.

Some ideas are just loud. Some are clever but soulless. Some are fun but forgettable.

So how do you know when an idea's worth doing? When it's more than just a flash of novelty? When it has legs and heart?

That's where the next framework comes in.

Because WoMBAT is the engine of discovery , it helps you generate a hundred ideas.

Laugh / Think / Cry is the filter , the emotional sniff test that helps you pick the right ones.

Together, they form the creative process I've used my entire career: one part imagination, one part gut check.

So if you've ever wondered "Is this idea good?" or "Is this worth the risk?" , this next chapter is for you.

TWO RANDOM THINGS without explanation that we worked on and they still make me laugh:

For the gentleman who doesn't care to wait.

Available Christmas 2018 because it's a gift.

Amber ALERT LAGER

amberalertlager.com

laugh, think, cry: the creative filter that guides everything

I HAVE A CONFESSION: I stole my core creative framework from a dying basketball coach. Well, borrowed is a nicer way to put it. It was the early '90s and I was watching legendary NCAA coach Jim "Jimmy V" Valvano give a speech shortly before cancer took his life. His words reached out from the TV and slapped me across the face. Jimmy V said there are three things we should do every day: laugh, think, and cry. "If you laugh, you think, and you cry, that's a full day... you do that seven days a week, you're going to have something special," he declared.

Here was a man with weeks to live, distilling life down to a simple, powerful idea: a day without laughter, thought, or emotion is a day wasted.

That hit me hard. At the time, I was a young buck in marketing, desperately trying to crack the code for what makes ideas stick. I realized this was the code. If a day isn't complete without laughter, thought, or tears, then maybe a marketing idea isn't complete without evoking one of those reactions.

Laugh, Think, Cry became more than just Jimmy's advice for a meaningful life, it became my litmus test for a meaningful idea. From that moment, every concept I came up with had to pass the Laugh/Think/Cry filter. If it didn't make you laugh, make you think, or make you feel something so deeply you might cry (tears of joy or sadness), then I knew it wasn't good enough. Harsh? Maybe. But in a world congested with boring, forgettable campaigns, I decided any idea that didn't hit two of those emotional marks was destined for the scrap heap. This wasn't some high-minded theory; it was a gut-check rule born out of a very real, very emotional moment for me. And it's guided my work ever since.

Fast forward to today: I'm known as "the smartest man in the world" in marketing circles. I've built high-profile brands, run word-of-mouth stunts that made journalists spit coffee through their noses, and helped companies win fans for life. People ask me all the time, "Saul, where do your crazy ideas come from? What's the secret sauce?" I tell them it's not where the ideas come from, it's how I judge them.

My secret sauce is a simple question I apply to every concept: Does it make someone laugh, think, or cry? If the answer is no, I go back to the drawing board. No matter how clever or cool an idea seems, if it doesn't trigger an emotional reaction, it's not going to get talked about. Period. All ideas must make people laugh, think, or cry, actually they have to make people feel two, or hell, go for the hat trick and get all three. That's my mantra. I even plastered those three words on my office wall in giant letters as a constant reminder (in case I get a swelled head and start thinking I can coast on "pretty good" ideas).

In this chapter, I'm going to break down each of the three pillars, Laugh, Think, Cry, and show you why they matter so damn much in marketing and creative work. I'll dive into the psychology and neuroscience that explain why emotion is the not-so-secret fuel behind attention, memory, decision-making, and the holy grail: sharing behavior. This isn't squishy "trust your feelings" stuff; it's backed by research and real-world results. By the end, I hope to convince you that if your idea doesn't make your audience laugh, think, or cry, if it doesn't move them in some way, then you should mercilessly kill that idea before it wastes a dime of your budget. Bold? Yes. Irreverent? Sure. But if there's one thing I've learned being the self-appointed smartest man in the world, it's that playing it safe is a shortcut to being ignored. And being ignored, my friends, is the kiss of death in marketing. So let's unpack Laugh/Think/Cry and why these three little words are the foundation of every big idea I've ever loved.

Laugh – The Power of Humor

I'm a firm believer that funny = money. Getting someone to laugh is like a marketing superpower, it breaks down walls, grabs attention, and if you're really good, it can even open wallets. Think about the last truly funny ad or campaign you saw. You probably still remember it, right? Maybe it was a Super Bowl commercial that had you and your friends cackling, or a viral TikTok from a brand that was so on-point you had to share it. That reaction is gold. In a world where consumers are blasted with thousands of ads a day, humor is a damn good way to stand out. Laughter makes people feel good, and people naturally gravitate toward things that make them feel good – including brands.

There's a reason I often push clients to inject some wit or absurdity into their campaigns. It's not because I want to audition for a Netflix comedy special, it's because humor works on a psychological level. When we experience laughter, our brains release dopamine, a feel-good neurotransmitter that's also linked to motivation and memory. That little dopamine hit essentially rewards your audience for paying attention to your message. They're more likely to remember what made them laugh. In fact, research shows that 90% of consumers are more likely to recall a product or brand if the advertisement is funny. Ninety percent! If that stat doesn't make you smirk, consider this: the same research found 72% of consumers would choose a brand that uses humor over a competitor's brand, and 80% say they're more likely to buy again if the brand consistently uses humor. Read that again and let it sink in, humor isn't just window dressing, it drives preference and repeat business.

And it's not just one study. A mountain of evidence backs up what our gut already knows: when people laugh, they listen and they share. A 2018 research paper found that humor in ads has a positive, strong effect on both word-of-mouth and ad recall. In other words, funny ads get people talking to each other (free advertising, anyone?) and help cement the brand in their memory banks. This makes perfect sense, when you see something hilarious, what's the first thing you want to do? You want to tell your friends, "Check this out!" Because making someone laugh feels good for you too; it boosts your social capital. Humor basically turns your audience into volunteer marketers, spreading your message for you. (Thank you, laughter, you overachiever.)

Now, let me clarify: using humour in marketing is not about turning your brand into a stand-up comedian or forcing jokes where they don't fit. It's about humanizing your message and meeting people on a common ground. Laughter is universal (okay, mostly universal, there's always that one guy with no sense of humor in the room). A well-placed joke or a clever bit of copy can disarm skepticism. It shows your audience that you don't take yourself too seriously and that you actually "get it." In an age of corporate-speak and buzz-word baloney, cracking a joke is like saying, "Hey, we're all humans here, let's have some fun." That builds trust and lika-bility, which are precursors to any positive customer action.

Of course, being funny in marketing is hard. For every brilliantly funny campaign, there are a dozen cringey ones. Timing, relevance, and brand voice all matter. You can't just meme your way to brand glory without understanding your audience's humor. And context is key, a joke that kills on Twitter (I don't really use twitter anymore but it will always be twitter to me) might bomb in a boardroom presentation. But the risk of not being funny is you become wallpaper. Bland. Forgettable. I'd rather shoot my shot with a bold, funny idea that 10% of people don't get than be instantly ignored by 100% because I played it safe. Boldness gets remembered; beige gets ignored. A running joke I make in some presentations is that I ask the audience "where were you when you first heard The Zodiac Album from Rudy Ray Moore" and show the album cover with Rudy and a woman completly naked. Is it in good taste? I don't know but it always makes me laugh.

Nudity aside, here are some quick-hit facts on humor's impact in marketing (show these to your boss next time they're afraid to approve the funny idea):

Attention & Recall: Funny content sticks. Ads using humor are significantly more likely to be remembered than their serious counterparts. Laughter triggers emotional arousal which boosts memory encoding, meaning your brand won't be forgotten five seconds after the ad ends.

Brand Affinity: Humor can literally make people like you. 72% of consumers favor the brand that makes them laugh, all else being equal. Positive emotions towards an ad transfer to positive feelings about the brand, a phenomenon ad researchers have observed for decades. In short, make 'em laugh and they'll love you (or at least like you more).

Social Sharing: Humorous content is more viral. One study of online articles found that content evoking amusement or surprise was far more likely to be shared, while downer content was less so. High-arousal positive emotions, like a good laugh, drive people to hit that share button. When we care, we share, and humor makes us care by entertaining us.

Purchase Intent: Laughter can lubricate the path to purchase. That Oracle study I cited earlier found 80% of people are likelier to buy again if a brand keeps them smiling.

Additionally, humor builds word-of-mouth (WOM) momentum, which is marketing code for "sales from free referrals." People love to pass along a funny recommendation. As one paper put it plainly: Humor in ads creates strong positive WOM and can indirectly boost sales via improved attitudes.

Let's talk examples. Some of the most iconic campaigns of all time leaned on laughter. Remember Old Spice's "The Man Your Man Could Smell Like" ads? Completely ridiculous, over-the-top – and utterly unforgettable. You laughed, you quoted it ("I'm on a horse"), and importantly, you remembered it was Old Spice. That campaign took a boring product (men's body wash) and made it a water-cooler conversation piece. Or consider Dollar Shave Club's launch video – the CEO strolling through a warehouse dropping one-liners like "Our blades are fucking great." (Bold for a razor company!) It went viral in hours. Millions watched and laughed, and Dollar Shave Club gained 12,000 customers in 48 hours, eventually disrupting an entire industry. The lesson: humor can transform the mundane into the talk of the town.

The real magic of Laugh as a filter is this: if an idea can make even one person laugh out loud, it's likely going to capture attention in a crowded media landscape. Laughter is an instant sign of engagement, you've broken through their mental spam filter and connected. And that's step one to doing anything meaningful. As a bonus, laughing together creates a mini-bond. Share a laugh with your audience and suddenly you're not just another company trying to sell something; you're the cool friend who told them a joke. That feeling can translate into loyalty over time. People want to keep around those who make them laugh, why wouldn't that apply to brands?

Before we move on, let me address the inevitable naysayer in the back: "But Saul, what if our business is super serious? We can't just crack jokes!" Look, I'm not telling the IRS to start doing stand-up routines (although…the CIA and FBI have posted a few jokes on social media and got a great response).

Not every brand can or should use overt humor. But every brand can benefit from being more human. Maybe that means a light touch of wit, or a clever metaphor, or just smiling in your messaging. The spirit of "Laugh" is about joy and delight, not punchlines per minute.

Even B2B brands have hearts (deep, deep down). I've seen enterprise software companies do tongue-in-cheek campaigns that made their customers smile and think, "Hey, these guys aren't a bunch of boring suits after all." And guess what, those customers picked up the phone. Being serious about your work doesn't mean you have to be solemn in your marketing.

Bottom line: humor is a high-reward strategy when done right. It's not the only way to win hearts, but it's one of the fastest. If an idea in your brainstorm has the potential to make someone laugh, pay attention, you might be onto something big. And if you're too scared to let your brand have a sense of humor, well, enjoy blending in with the 10,000 other forgettable messages people see today. As for me, I'll be over here betting on laughter and reaping the rewards. Laugh, and the world laughs with you, and maybe buys your product, too.

Think – The Reward of Intellectual Stimulation

"Make them think" might sound odd in a marketing context. A lot of advertisers assume consumers don't want to think, they're wrong. People love to learn, to be intrigued, to have their curiosity piqued. The Think pillar of my framework is all about ideas that engage the audience's intellect or imagination. We're talking about the kind of content that makes you go, "Huh, I never thought of it that way," or "Wow, that's interesting, tell me more." This could be a clever twist in a campaign, a provocative question posed by a brand, an insight that makes you pause and reflect, or a novel concept that blows your mind. In a nutshell, Think is about intellectual and creative stimulation, lighting up the brain in ways beyond a quick laugh or a cheap tear-jerker.

From a neurological perspective, Think is a powerhouse. When you present people with something novel or thought-provoking, you're activating their brain's reward circuitry. New and surprising information triggers the release of dopamine in the hippocampus, which promotes memory formation. In plain English: novel ideas stick. Our brains are evolutionarily wired to latch onto things that are different or unexpected, because those could be important for survival. Now, in modern times, "important for survival" might be reinterpreted as "important enough to share with my friends or act on." If you can make someone scratch their head (in a good way) or lean forward in intrigue, you've got their attention on lock. Surprise is literally a physiological "wake-up" call to the brain, it spikes norepinephrine (our alertness chemical) which heightens focus and helps sear the moment into memory. Ever wonder why you remember odd, random facts or the twist ending of a movie? Because the element of surprise jolted your brain into paying full attention. In marketing, a well-crafted idea that makes people think different or reframe something can have the same effect.

Consider campaigns that reveal a shocking statistic or present an unexpected comparison. Those "#LikeAGirl" ads by Always, for example, flipped a common insult on its head and made viewers rethink their biases, you watch that and you think about how language affects self-esteem. Or take the classic Apple "1984" ad, it made you think about computers as tools of empowerment versus conformity. It basically said, think different (literally their later tagline). That ad didn't have a joke, it didn't make you cry; it made you consider a new perspective (and damn, did it make an impact, effectively launching the Mac with an ethos).

The Think category often overlaps with concepts like awe, wonder, and surprise. These are emotions too, but they're tied to cognition. Marketing Professor Jonah Berger analyzed thousands of New York Times articles to figure out what went viral. He found that articles which evoked awe, a sense of wonder or fascinating insight, were highly likely to make the "most emailed" list. People share content that makes them feel high-arousal positive emotions, which awe and excitement from learning something new definitely qualify as. Another key driver was practical value, content that made you think "This is useful, I should pass it on." The common thread is that our brains light up at content that is either useful, novel, or intellectually satisfying. We like feeling smart and we like sharing things that make us look smart or enlightened to others. (Go on, admit it, you've forwarded an interesting article to a friend or posted a cool fact on LinkedIn to seem 10% smarter. We all have.)

From a marketing standpoint, making your audience think can mean several things: maybe your ad has a clever twist that isn't immediately obvious, so the viewer gets a little aha! moment when they figure it out. That micro-second of problem-solving is rewarding , it gives the audience a sense of satisfaction and involvement. Or maybe your campaign educates the audience on an issue in a novel way, effectively teaching them without feeling like a lecture. That builds goodwill and positions your brand as thoughtful. Or perhaps you present a bold insight or stance that challenges conventional thinking, something that makes people stop and say,

"Wait, they're right (or they're crazy)... either way I'm thinking about it." That can spur conversation and debate, which again keeps your brand in the mix.

One of my favorite ways to invoke Think is through surprise and reframing. Show the audience something familiar, then flip it. Or surprise them with a contrast. There's a psychological reason for this: as mentioned, surprise triggers intense focus and memory encoding. There's a great term in psychology, "schema violation." It basically means you break the expected pattern. When an ad plays out differently than people assumed, it forces them to engage more deeply to reconcile the surprise. They think about it longer. And that extra thought is the point, it means they're spending more time with your idea (more mental impressions = more likely to remember and act on it).

Let me drop a spicy truth here: most marketing doesn't respect the audience's intelligence. This industry has a bad habit of dumbing things down, spoon-feeding, or oversimplifying.

And sure, clarity is key, I'm not advocating riddles for the sake of being obtuse. But when you treat people like they have a brain (because, newsflash, they do) and invite them to use it, they appreciate it. They become participants in the idea, not just passive receivers. That participation can be as small as figuring out a joke (laughter often has a think component via surprise), or as deep as pondering a story or message long after the ad is over.

The neuroscience backs this up beyond just surprise. Studies show that when people are intellectually engaged, they enter a state of focused attention that actually creates stronger memory traces. They're not just hearing your message, they're processing it. If humor is a quick hit of dopamine, intellectual stimulation is more like a slow drip, it keeps people engrossed. They might spend an extra minute reading your ad or replaying your video to catch nuances. That extra time and mental effort is marketing gold, because it means your idea is sinking in deeper. There's even evidence that novel, challenging experiences trigger reward pathways similar to enjoyment, learning can be inherently pleasurable for the brain, releasing dopamine much like laughter does. Ever do a puzzle or trivia and feel that little rush when you get it right? That's the brain's reward for thinking. Good marketing can tap into that too.

Let's look at how Think translates in real campaigns. The classic example: "Got Milk?" ads, they posed a question and let you figure out the answer (why you need milk, because a mouthful of dry peanut butter sandwich without it is torture). It engaged your mind with a problem-solution format. Or more modern: those Spotify year-end "Wrapped" campaigns with clever data insights ("You streamed 4,000 minutes of Neal Hamburger, you were in the top 1% of his fans"). People eat that stuff up because it's interesting info about them, it makes them think and then proudly share the quirky facts. Another one: a few years back, a UK road safety campaign for cyclists used an awareness test ("Count how many passes the team in white makes") and most viewers missed the moon-walking bear in the video, the tagline: "It's easy to miss some-thing you're not looking for." It forced the viewer to think and realize they had a blind spot, delivering the safety message in a way that made you slap your forehead. You can bet that stuck in people's heads far more than a typical "be careful, drivers!" PSA.

Campaigns that make you think often also give you some-thing to talk about. When a brand provides a compelling insight or a "Did you know?" nugget, audiences become ambassadors, eager to share the newfound knowledge. Curiosity and awe are highly shareable emotions, we share what fascinates or enlightens us, not just what amuses or angers us. Look at the popularity of TED Talks or interesting infographics on social media. When a company shares a mind-blowing statistic or a new way to view a common issue, that content gets reposted with captions like "Whoa, never realized this." That's word-of-mouth being driven by the Think factor.

However, a word of caution: to make people think, you still have to meet them where they are. If you confuse them or go too high-brow, you lose them. The key is to challenge the audience just the right amount, enough to engage, not so much that they give up. The sweet spot is what psychologists call desirable difficulty. It's like a riddle that's solvable with a bit of effort, satisfying to crack but not impossible. The same goes for marketing. Don't make your message so subtle or complex that only PhDs get it. But don't insult our intelligence by spelling out the moral of the story in skywriting either. Find that middle ground where the audience can join the dots and feel smart for doing so.

When a campaign nails this, the impact goes beyond just recall or sharing, it can actually influence decision-making on a deeper level. If you've successfully made someone think differently about a topic (say, the importance of your product or a cause you're highlighting), that cognitive shift can lead to a change in behavior. For example, a sustainability campaign that uses a clever visual to make you think about plastic waste in a new way may actually convince you to start using a reusable water bottle. You didn't cry, you didn't laugh, but the idea stuck in your head and changed you. As a marketer, that's a huge win.

To sum up the Think pillar: An idea that engages the brain will gain a place in the brain. If you can intrigue your audience, educate them, surprise them, or get them pondering a question, you've given them more than an advertisement, you've given them an experience. And experiences, especially mentally stimulating ones, tend to get stored in memory and shared in conversation. So ask yourself in your creative process: does this idea just wash over people, or does it make them pause and think? If it's the latter, you're on the right track to something shareable and impactful.

Cry – The Pull of Emotional Resonance

Now we come to Cry, the big emotional kahuna. Out of the three, this is the one that gets closest to the heart. When I say "cry," I don't literally mean every campaign should have people bawling their eyes out (though if you can genuinely move someone to tears and still tie it to your brand, you're probably winning). Cry is shorthand for emotional resonance: content that tugs at heartstrings, gives you goosebumps, inspires you, or connects on a deeply human level. It's the kind of idea that might make your voice catch in your throat or send a shiver down your spine. We're talking meaningful emotion, joy, love, sadness, hope, anger at injustice, pride, triumph, solidarity. This is the stuff that makes people feel alive and often, it's the foundation of word-of-mouth magic.

Humans are emotional creatures first and rational creatures second. Don't believe me? Consider this finding: Emotions are strongly correlated with attention, decision-making, and memory. In fact, neuroscientists have argued that emotions are not just useful but necessary for decision-making and for memories to stick. We remember things that had an emotional impact; we make choices based on how we feel and justify them later with logic. This is as true for choosing a brand of soda as it is for choosing a life partner (though please, don't make love to a soda can, it's weird). For advertising, this means if you want your message to sink in and influence behavior, you'd better speak to the heart, not just the head.

Emotional advertising has a stellar track record. One huge analysis of 1,400 successful ad campaigns found that purely emotional campaigns were about twice as effective as rational ones (31% vs 16%). Read that again: double the effectiveness.

Even mixing emotional and rational content outperformed straight rational messaging. Why? Because emotion engages. It cuts through the noise. It lights up the brain's limbic system, creating a flashbulb memory. An old study (by Page et al., 1990) noted that ads with emotional content are more likely to be remembered than ads conveying only information. And that was observed way back then, long before the current era of content overload, it's even more true now. Emotional resonance gives your idea staying power.

Let's break down what happens when you hit the Cry button in someone's psyche. Imagine a touching story in an ad, say a short film about a father and daughter that makes you tear up, or an inspirational montage of people overcoming odds. What's happening in your brain? A couple of big neurochemicals are at play: cortisol and oxytocin. Cortisol is a stress hormone that, in the right doses, focuses your attention. A compelling emotional narrative will often raise cortisol a bit – if you feel anxious or distressed for the characters, you're glued to the screen. Oxytocin is the famed "love hormone" or empathy chemical; it surges when we feel connected or moved by others. The more empathetic you feel, the more oxytocin is released.

Dr. Paul Zak, a neuroeconomist, has done fascinating studies on this. In one experiment, participants watched an emotional story about a terminally ill child. The result: their cortisol and oxytocin levels spiked, and those with higher oxytocin levels (i.e., who felt more empathy) donated significantly more money to charity right after. In fact, Zak's team could predict who would donate just by measuring oxytocin in the blood. That's wild. Emotional resonance literally changed behavior, people opened their wallets because their hearts were touched. If that doesn't convince you of emotion's power, I don't know what will.

What's beautiful about the Cry category is that it covers a spectrum of feelings. It could be happy tears too, like those videos of soldiers returning home that make you sob out of pure joy. (I'm not crying, you're crying.) Jimmy V himself clarified "cry" as having your emotions moved to tears, could be happiness or joy. So in marketing, an emotionally resonant piece could be upbeat and inspiring (think of those tear-jerking Olympic athlete profiles backed by triumphant music that leave you feeling uplifted and ready to hug the nearest flag). Or it could be a poignant, somber message that calls attention to a problem (think public service announcements or cause-related campaigns that haunt you with a real, human story). The key is authenticity. Audiences can smell fake senti-mentality a mile away. Slapping a sad soundtrack on a shallow story won't do anything. You have to mean it. The story or message has to hold genuine emotional truth.

When an idea hits the Cry criterion, it tends to go beyond marketing and enters culture. These are the campaigns people talk about years later. Look at the Thai life insurance commer-cials that go viral globally every few years, no jokes, no gimmicks, just powerful mini-stories about kindness that leave you sobbing and oddly feeling good about humanity (and by extension, that insurance brand). Or consider Don Draper's legendary ad for Coca-Cola's "Hilltop, I'd like to buy the world a Coke" ad. It doesn't make you cry, per se, but it generates a warm fuzzy feeling of global unity and peace. People remember that decades on, because it wasn't selling delicious zero sugar water, it was selling a positive emotion, a moment. Emotional resonance gives your idea a long tail. People might forget the exact details, but they remember how it made them feel, and by association, they remember you. As the famous Maya Angelou quote goes (which I'll paraphrase): People will forget what you said, people will forget what you did, but people will never forget Saul Colt made them feel. Brands that capitalize on that truth create loyal fans.

Emotion is also the bedrock of word-of-mouth. Why do we share anything with others? Often, it's because it made us feel something strongly and we want to pass that feeling on. According to research on social sharing, when we share content, we're not just sharing the content, we're sharing the emotional experience it gave us. If a video gave you chills or had you choking up, you share it because you want your friend to experience that punch in the heart too. Emotional contagion is real; we are social creatures who sync our feelings. A study of the most-shared ads found that the top ones all carried strong emotional themes, friendship, inspiration, happiness. Even in the age of cynical internet culture, heartwarming and heartfelt content consistently rises above the noise. It's telling that some of the most viral content ever (think Susan Boyle's first audition on Britain's Got Talent, which made millions of people cry happy tears and share like crazy, not me but millions of others) had nothing to do with a product but everything to do with emotional impact. Smart brands latch onto those human stories and align themselves with that energy.

Now, a pitfall to avoid: emotional manipulation. Cry is powerful, but with great power comes great responsibility (thanks, Uncle Ben…Spider-Man not rice). If an audience feels manipulated, like you're twisting their emotions just to sell them something, it can backfire spectacularly. People don't like feeling like their heartstrings are being yanked for cash. The emotion has to serve a genuine narrative or value. For instance, those Sarah McLachlan ASPCA ads with the abused animals and the heartbreaking song? They're essentially weaponized sadness. Maybe highly effective for driving donations, but many people also resent them for being so emotionally heavy-handed. In a commercial context, if you're going to make people cry, you need to earn it with substance and sincerity. The story should stand on its own legs, with the brand a natural part of it, not a tacky logo slapped at the end of a mini tearjerker film. When done right, emotional marketing can build immense goodwill, people feel like the brand "gets" them and stands for something more. When done wrong, it feels like cheap exploitation….like that weird Super Bowl ad with the kid dying in a bathtub for Nationwide Insurance. That was crazy and manipulative,

One more fascinating facet: emotional resonance can create a community. When an idea strikes an emotional chord, it often unites people who felt that same way. That's how you get movements. A campaign that highlights, say, everyday heroes (teachers, nurses, me, etc.) might rally people around appreciating those folks. Everyone who shared that content is subtly bonding over a shared value or feeling. This is where marketing transcends into something like community-building. And the brand that facilitated that feeling? They earn a seat at the table of that emerging community. That's deeper than engagement; that's belonging, which is among the strongest human drives.

Bringing it back to marketing objectives: emotional campaigns build brand equity in a profound way. They might not always drive an immediate sale ("Aww, that ad made me cry, I'm gonna go buy dead kid insurance right now!" isn't a typical consumer response). But they shape perception and affinity. They make your brand the one that stands for the things people care about. Over time, that's what creates advocates and evangelists. People will forgive a company's missteps if they've developed an emotional bond with its stories and values. It's like any relationship, loaded with feeling. And frankly, a lot of purchasing is emotional anyway. We choose the brands that make us feel confident, cool, safe, or happy. So why not design our marketing to deliver those feelings upfront?

Alright, let's recap with some knowledge nuggets on Cry and emotional resonance:

Memory & Recall: Emotions burn memories into our brains. High emotional arousal (whether joy or sadness) flags the experience as important. No surprise, then, that emotional ads imprint stronger memories than neutral ones, making your brand message last longer in people's minds.

Decision Impact: Feelings guide decisions. We often decide based on emotion and backfill with logic. Creating an emotional connection means your brand will feel like the right choice when the moment comes. In one study, emotional response to ads was found to be a better predictor of sales than the ad's content itself, showing just how crucial the feeling is.

Virality & Sharing: Passion is contagious. Content that makes people feel intensely (uplifted, outraged, heartbroken, inspired) is content people share. Research confirms a strong relationship between emotional intensity and virality. In fact, emotions, positive or negative, underlie most viral phenomena. A moving story or an inspiring message has a built-in shareability, because we crave that shared emotional experience.

Brand Loyalty: Emotional resonance creates loyalists. When a brand consistently connects with an audience's values and feelings, it graduates from purveyor of goods to trusted friend or inspirational leader. That's how you get life-long customers and word-of-mouth ambassadors. As an example, think of brands like Nike: their ads often aim for inspiration (think of the "If you let me play sports" campaign, it hit you in the gut with emotion and conviction). That emotional boldness alienated some, but bonded many to Nike's brand ethos even tighter.

In my experience, an idea that nails the Cry factor is an idea that will not only be talked about, but felt in the cultural zeitgeist. Those are the ideas that win awards, sure, but more importantly they win hearts. And when you win hearts, wallets follow.

Hitting All Three: The Ultimate Creative Test

Here's the holy grail: the rare idea that makes you laugh, think, and cry. These are the home runs, the "we're gonna reference this in marketing textbooks" campaigns. Do you need all three every time?

No.

Hitting one in my opinion is not enough but hitting two is the goal. When you manage to touch all three emotional triggers in one go, you've got something epic on your hands. It's the kind of transcendent storytelling that Pixar masters in movies (one minute you're laughing, next you're contemplating life, next you're sobbing).

In our world, that might look like a campaign that uses humor to draw you in, delivers a thought-provoking message, and leaves you with an emotional payoff. It's hard to pull off, but boy, when it works, you've created a moment people will never forget.

The Laugh/Think/Cry filter isn't just a catchy slogan, it's a discipline. It forces you to ask of every idea: what's the emotional core? If there isn't one, you have permission to kill that darling and move on. This keeps you honest. Early in my career, I'd sometimes fall in love with an idea that was "cool" or visually impressive or super clever. But if I really examined it, there was no emotional substance, it wouldn't make anyone laugh, think, or cry. It was an empty calorie. By holding everything to this standard, you avoid the trap of superficial gimmicks. You zero in on what will genuinely connect with an audience.

I'm not saying every piece of content needs to be a tearjerker or a knee-slapper or galaxy-brain revelation. But it needs to be at least Two of those. There are too many options and messages competing for your audience's time. If you're not evoking any strong reaction, you're evoking indifference, and indifference is the enemy of marketing. Apathetic viewers don't remember, don't engage, don't buy, and certainly don't share. As a creative or marketer, you should rather someone absolutely love or even hate your campaign than shrug their shoulders and forget it in five seconds. Love and hate are two sides of the same coin: passion. And passion spreads. A shrug is a dead end.

Emotional resonance, in whichever form (humor, intellectual engagement, heartfelt connection), is truly the foundation of word-of-mouth. When people are moved, they move others. Think of the last time you wouldn't shut up about a show, an ad, or a news story, it's because it hit an emotional nerve for you. That's exactly what we want our ideas to do. It's the difference between a campaign that fizzles after the media spend is done and one that keeps echoing because people carry it forward in conversation, social media, and personal recommendations.

If you're a marketer, creative, brand builder, whatever, the challenge I pose to you is to adopt this filter in your own work. When you're brainstorming, literally write "Laugh, Think, Cry" on the whiteboard (I do, it freaks clients out at first and then they get it).

Pressure test each concept: Which box (or boxes) does this tick? If none, have the guts to say, "Next idea, please." It's a game-changer when you start thinking this way. Your batting average for big hits will improve. You'll start naturally gravitating towards ideas that have heart, wit, or brains (or all). And you'll quickly spot the hollow stuff that might look shiny but won't make a dent in anyone's day.

Let me be clear: this framework isn't about being sappy or jokey or brainy for the sake of it. It's about respecting the audience's humanity. Laugh acknowledges that people love to be delighted. Think acknowledges that people love to be intrigued. Cry acknowledges that people love to feel something real. You give them one (or more) of these experiences, and in return they'll give you their attention, their memory space, their loyalty, and maybe even their money.

Fair trade, if you ask me.

And hey, if you can hit all three in one fell swoop, do it! But even the attempt to cover two tends to elevate an idea. Don't force it if it's not there, but challenge yourself to layer dimensions. Maybe your humorous idea can carry a subtle insightful message (laugh + think). Maybe your serious emotional story can have a moment of levity to make the characters more relatable (cry + laugh). Maybe your thought-leadership piece can include an anecdote that tugs the heartstrings (think + cry). When you start blending these elements, you create richness. It's like cooking, sweet, salty, umami, etc. The right combo makes a dish unforgettable. Same with creative ingredients.

At the end of the day, an idea that makes people feel something is an idea that will be talked about. We share emotions, not facts and features. No one ever said, "You've got to see this ad, it has great slide transitions and a really thorough list of product specs!" (If they did, they might be a robot.) But they do say, "You've got to see this – it's hilarious," or "…it's shocking," or "…it's so touching." That's the stuff that spreads. That's word-of-mouth fertilizer.

So here's the bold, irreverent, unfiltered Saul Colt challenge: If your idea doesn't make someone laugh, or think, or cry, preferably two out of three, and on a great day all three, then do us all a favor and put it in the garbage. Don't ship mediocrity. The world has enough noise. Aim for impact. Aim to be the thing people talk about at the bar or share at the meeting or post on their feed with a "THIS 👇" caption. That's the bar you should set for yourself, every time.

Laugh. Think. Cry. It's a simple filter, but it's saved me from green-lighting a lot of lukewarm crap over the years. It's made my work braver and more effective. It's why some folks have called me a word-of-mouth marketing guru (though I prefer "prophet of awesome," if we're choosing titles). But honestly, there's nothing mystical about it. It's just about remembering what matters to people at a fundamental level. We want to feel something, to be entertained, to be intrigued, to be moved. Do that, and you've done your job as a communicator.

Jimmy V gave me the words to articulate what I long suspected. I'll always be grateful to him for dying (see what I did there...jokes people) and giving that final speech and the gift of Laugh, Think, Cry. If he were here, I'd like to think he'd get a kick out of how a marketing guy twisted his life lesson into an advertising mantra. I took "That's a full day" and turned it into "That's a damn good campaign." Different context, same truth. Emotion is life. Emotion is marketing. Emotion is everything.

Now go forth and create something worth laughing about, worth thinking about, or worth crying about, ideally all of the above. That's how you make sure your work means something to people. And if it means something, they'll remember it and share it.

Every. Single. Time.

In summary: Make 'em laugh, make 'em think, make 'em cry, or else what the hell are you even doing?

8 /
the bold and the brainy: selling audacious ideas to the risk-averse

PICTURE THIS: me, a Zoom call with a Fortune 100 marketing honcho, and your wild idea on the line. The executive told me it was "the greatest idea ever pitched... exactly what we should be doing, but we're not going to do it." I asked why. The exec basically shrugged: "I make about $350,000 a year... another million in bonuses, I will never find another gig like this so why would I risk it?"

End of story.

In other words, it wasn't about ROI, it was a straight "cover your ass" play. The sad truth is, most people gut-check creative ideas with fear, not excitement. Human beings are literally hardwired to protect what's familiar. Pitching a crazy idea often feels risky to them, so you have to pitch it differently. Instead of bragging only about the upside, frame it as avoiding a brutal downside. Remember: we feel losses twice as strongly as we feel gains. So tell them what happens if you don't do it. "If we sit this out, we'll be the dinosaurs , not the Tyrannosaurus." Now that will sting harder than "we might make an extra 10%."

The truth is, bold, out-there ideas make 7 out of 10 clients flinch. CEOs love them in theory, hate them in practice. But in today's crowded CPG, tech, and fashion markets, playing it safe is a guaranteed way to be forgotten. In fact, with **500,000 brands** across thousands of categories and 30,000 new products each year there is still a 95% flop rate. Capturing attention takes more than another vanilla PowerPoint. It takes guts, science, and a killer pitch. Welcome to the crash course in getting your colleagues and clients to say "Hell yes" to your wildest schemes.

Why Change Feels Like Holding a Python

First, let's diagnose the fear. Humans have **giant** built in defenses against change. Behavioral science calls it **status quo bias**: we **love** keeping things exactly as they are, even if it's not ideal. Change is literally scarier to our brain than losing a treasured $20.

Loss aversion teaches us why: studies show the pain of giving something up is about **twice** as powerful as the joy of gaining the same thing. That means a client sees your bold idea not as a potential gain, but as a threat to what they already have. "What if this fails?" becomes louder than "What if this conquers the world?"

Put simply: doing nothing feels **safer**, even when the cost of "same old" is painful. No wonder 40% of sales pitches sputter out in indecision. The client isn't evil or stupid; their lizard brain simply craves certainty. One sales analysis bluntly notes, **"When a customer decides not to do anything…they are maintaining the status quo."** That's our uphill battle.

And there are layers of panic on top of panic. The decision makers fret about **brand damage, budget blame, and shareholder explosions**. They think, "If this crashes and burns, I'm toast!" Ego and liability loom over every risk. Meanwhile, practical barriers , tight timelines, legal red tape, missing data , stack up like a hostile boardroom jury. Emotional fears and real constraints combine to form a perfect "DANGER: DO NOT CROSS" sign in everyone's mind.

The key to selling your mad vision is to dismantle these

fears one by one. You have to reframe the story, hold their hand through the data, and even sneakily shift their thinking with psychology.

Reframing Reality: Framing, Stories, and Social Proof

Enter the persuasion playbook. Bad ideas latch onto fear; great pitches use brain tricks to shift perspective. One classic move is **framing**. Remember those health brochures about breast exams? When women were told **"If you don't self-examine, you could die of cancer"** (loss framing), they reacted much more strongly than if the brochure said "If you self-examine, you stay healthy" (gain framing). Don't panic your client with doom about unsubtle change ("your business will sink without this"), but do highlight what they stand to **lose** by standing still: shrinking market share, fading brand relevance, lost sales. Make it visceral: "Every quarter you wait, you bleed X% to competitors." That "cost of inaction" hits the primal brain. In fact, one sales guide advises quantifying **doing nothing**, because showing the **price** of staying put can jolt clients into action.

Next, **social proof**. Even tough executives fall prey to it. Someone I respect greatly, Robert Cialdini defines social proof as people doing what they **see** others doing. If it's convincing that other brands (especially similar ones) took a leap, your client's inner auditor will dial down. Pitch it like: "Look, Nike just went all-in on social justice with Kaepernick's face on billboards, and their sales jumped 31% over a weekend. If Nike can lean into controversy, maybe you can, too." Show them trendy case studies or competitor campaigns. A classic story: place an ad in an industry mag listing major peers who did it. People will think, "All the cool kids are doing it, what am I missing?" (Just be honest about who's really taken the risk.)

Then, **storytelling**. Neuroscientists love narratives because they glue us to the pitch. Story mode activates the listener's sympathy and imagination, taking pressure off them to parse every bullet point. A fun twist: researchers found that stories can actually **blind** people to weak facts. The takeaway? When your case is persuasive but a tad thin, tell a vivid tale. Paint a mini-saga: "Imagine Sarah, a 32-year-old shopper, scrolling through Instagram. She ignores bland ads until our viral video pops up, grabs her attention, and whispers in her ear to try our line…" The more engaged they are in the narrative, the less they'll nitpick the numbers. Derek Rucker of Kellogg summarizes:

> **"Stories can be fantastic; you might want to use them… However, there's a 'but'… a story can limit our ability to process facts."**

So lean into stories **when** the facts themselves aren't enough on their own. If you have rock-solid data, still wrap it in a story about a real customer or the brand's hero journey for maximum punch.

Other Cialdini tricks help, too.

Reciprocity: do you have a small gift to sweeten the pot? "We've done some unpaid market research for you already, here's a preview report." People hate feeling indebted, so even a little gesture can make them repay the favor by listening (and hopefully saying yes).

Authority and Liking: quote your credentials or bring a respected guru's opinion. Maybe a celebrity usage stat ("+30% after celebrity X used the product!") or a well-known agency case study. If a quirky department head **loves** you, have them mention you by name: if they **like** the idea, everyone else sneaks along.

Scarcity: it sounds counterintuitive, but even making an offer sound **limited** ("first 100 clients get this trial") can create a rush. And don't forget **commitment**: even a small "yes" earns goodwill. First get them to agree on a modest pilot

("Let's test a minimal version"), then later slide in the bigger ask.

At its heart, selling bold ideas is storytelling + social proof + a dash of brain chemistry. If you can cast their fear into a dramatic narrative and sprinkle in peer pressure, the skeptics start to soften. As one marketing CMO put it,

---

"Brave brands know what they stand for, and what they don't. These brands go beyond being different; they have a point of view, make a promise, and deliver on that promise."

That's our mantra: anchor boldness in the brand's authentic promise, so it doesn't feel like whimsy but like destiny.

Real-World Riveting (and Ruined) Pitches

Theory is fun, but nothing beats real campaigns for credibility. Let's dissect a few bold moves, hits and flops alike, especially from CPG, tech, and fashion.

Fearless Girl is one legendary case of pitching the unthinkable. In 2017 State Street Global Advisors (a financial firm) quietly decided to loudly advocate for women in leadership. They simply placed a bronze girl statue staring defiantly at the iconic Wall Street Bull. No safe slideshow, no polite ad, just art in the street on Women's Day, demanding boardroom change. Internally, imagine the pitch: "We plop this tiny girl in Manhattan, everyone talks about it, media galore, and we're on the side of empowering women." They backed it with data (60 companies already agreed to add female directors) and a promise of real investor funds.

The risk? Reputation and legal: the Charging Bull's sculptor got mad, New Yorkers got mad. But the **social proof** was instant, everyone knew or covered **Fearless Girl**. In 12 weeks she racked up billions of social-media impressions and helped push 152 companies to add women to their boards. That raw boldness tied directly to SSGA's purpose, so it felt **earned**. When pitches scared of backlash came up, the team reframed it:

"**If we don't do this, we'll never get heard. Sitting it out is the only unbrave thing.**"

Ultimately, the stunt was a splashy admission: "Yes, we're disrupting finance **and** advancing women." Even Mayor de Blasio and Forbes took notice. That's alignment (and story-telling) at its finest.

"Old Spice's "Man Your Man"

Remember the old-school aftershave ads? Sappy guys in white rooms, talking to camera. In 2010 P&G decided enough, and asked Wieden+Kennedy to "Target women, they buy 60% of our men's bodywash." So instead of nice music, W+K gave us a towel-clad hunk and a razor-sharp joke: **"Hello, ladies. Look at your man… now look at me… Now I'm on a horse."**. It sounds insane , and it was meant to be. The pitch was basically, "Let's be ridiculously memo-rable." The ad never even aired on Super Bowl TV (they cheekily dropped it online first). The result? By May 2010, **Red Zone** body-wash sales were up a whopping 60% (their goal had only been 15%). By summer, sales had **doubled**. That stunned everybody. They sold millions of units with a moustachioed pirate vibe and a fake game show. If you're afraid your client will think it's "too weird," point to this: P&G themselves wrote off Super Bowl prime time and still scored. The pitch, it turned out, was green-lit by math and giggles: women buy men's body wash, and women loved it too. The lesson: Break rigid brand rules if you give customers a reason to smile at the data (and profits) will follow.

Nike's "Dream Crazy":

Perhaps nothing in recent years was more polarizing than Nike's 2018 Colin Kaepernick ad. Here was a mainstream athletic brand, wagering on protestor-turned-icon. Internally, imagine the arguments: "Aligning with an NFL anthem protester will blow back!" Versus, "Our core buyers (millennial and Gen Z) will celebrate it. It screams authenticity."

Nike framed it as

"Believe in something. Even if it means sacrificing everything."

The boldness paid off , sales didn't dip, they surged. According to Edison Trends, Nike's online sales spiked **31%** immediately after launch, outpacing even the last Labor Day weekend. (Vox later reported Nike made an **extra $6 billion** since that campaign.) Despite presidential tweets calling it "a terrible message," consumers resonated with Nike's point of view. Nike sold conviction with shoes, proving that a righteous brand stand can trump fear of boycott.

Always "# LikeAGirl":

Another P&G winner: Always declared war on the phrase "like a girl" (long used as an insult). The team ran an emotional video: let girls do pushups **"like a girl"** and compare that to grown women doing it. The shift was immediate: what used to be an insult became a badge of confidence. Always tied this to their brand promise (empowerment), so it wasn't salesy at all. The campaign **hit hearts**: it racked up tens of millions of views worldwide and boosted Always's image among young women (and men). The concrete payoff: a 3% sales jump in its first year (for an already established product). The company made girls feel stronger and sold more tampons. Win-win.

Easter Eggs-Small Pitches, Big Wins:

Even in tech, daring sells. In 2006, IBM researcher David Ferrucci pitched a crazy idea: build a supercomputer that could **beat humans at Jeopardy!**. His bosses must have been skeptical, but he framed it as pushing IBM's AI limits. Five years later, Watson trounced trivia champion Ken Jennings on TV, giving IBM a PR victory and proving serious tech chops. No pie-charts needed, just a jaw-dropping demo. In pitching terms: Ferrucci sold the story of a machine that will talk your language better than Google, wrapped in a friendly quiz show battle.

Bold Flops – Learn by the Faceplants:

Not every radical pitch sticks the landing, and it's vital to own those lessons. Pepsi's 2017 Kendall Jenner ad is textbook. The pitch was "social protest unity." It went like:

"**Women march. Trendy model hands police officer a Pepsi. Problem solved.**"

People were horrified. As a Marsha P. Johnson Institute leader put it, the ad "plays down the sacrifices people have historically taken" in protests, adding **"no one is finding joy from Pepsi at a protest"**. Pepsi tried to flip a hot button, but the **audience fired first**. The lesson: shock value must be authentic, not cheap.

Gap's 2010 logo redesign is another: a subtle brand change pitched as "update for modern sensibilities" became a social media feeding frenzy. Within **six days** Gap scrapped the new logo after mockery and meme shame. Their pitch probably lacked customer input.

Moral: inviting stakeholders into the process beats forcing change overnight.

Burger King's sexist tweet stunt (UK, International Women's Day 2021) also flopped. The pitch: get attention with controversy. The first tweet said

---

"Women belong in the kitchen." - Burger King

Ouch. The follow-ups revealed it was for a culinary scholarship program. But many never saw the follow up tweets 1-2 days later, they only saw "Women belong in the kitchen" and got furious. The shock didn't hook them; it choked them. When your bait doesn't land, the whole campaign drowns.

I have never had one but I have heard that failures happen, if you have one use it as a lesson, not a life sentence. The key: analyze **why** the pitch tanked. (Was it tone-deaf? Mis-framed? Poor timing?) Then sell *__that__* story internally: "Look, we tried X, it backfired because of Y, so here's how we fix it." Showing you learned builds trust.

Clearing Emotional and Practical Hurdles

So we've scared them, sold them an alternative, and

showed examples. But even with all that, you'll hit two road-blocks: **emotions and details**.

Emotionally, your clients will wrestle with imposter syndrome: "What if **I'm** the one who championed the failed campaign?" Address this by sharing the risk. Admit out loud: "Yes, this is risky. If you want safety, we can do that beige campaign that gets ignored." Then pivot: "But here's the reward." Align the risk with outcomes they care about (growth, relevance, market share). Sometimes acknowledging fear disarms it. **Say something like, "I know this sounds nuts, I felt that too, but the upside is so much bigger than the cost of staying invisible."**

On the practical side, break it down. Budgets, resources, and tech constraints are easy objections. Solve them in the pitch itself: "We'll phase this, starting at 5% of the marketing budget for a test run." Or "We used existing assets, only minor edits needed, no million-dollar CGI." Have backup plans: "If regulation bites, we have Plan B campaign that leans on positive messaging instead." Demonstrate due diligence so they know you aren't blind to feasibility.

Team up with internal champions. Before the big meeting, get one sympathetic stakeholder on board. It could be a junior exec or the CFO who secretly dreams of something cool. Arm them with snippets of your story and data. Social proof works internally too: if they hear someone on **their** side advocating your idea, it chimes as consensus rather than just the mad pitch of one creative.

Show prototypes or concept boards, not just text. Tangible visuals turn "abstract crazy idea" into "almost-real thing." It's hard to deny pretty pictures and mockups. Even a quick storyboard video or mood board can make your idea feel concrete.

Finally, employ the **cost-of-inaction** wrap: prepare a one-pager that contrasts **two futures**: "A = current trajectory" vs "B = with our idea." Quantify where possible (dollars, brand metrics, user engagement) and highlight the gap. When clients see the **potential loss** of doing nothing, you turn loss-aversion on its head. They may hate risking money, but they hate leaving money on the table even more.

Bold Wins, Proof It Matters

By now it should be clear why this dance with risk is worth it. Brands that tiptoe never make headlines. Consider these stats: after Nike's controversial gamble, sales **grew** even under boycott threats. When Old Spice broke all the rules with humor, Red Zone body wash **doubled** sales. Edelman found **81%** of consumers buy from brands they trust and believe will act in their best interest. Trust and emotional resonance top buyers' lists. In fact, **83%** of CMOs worldwide say emotional connection is critical for their business future. Those aren't fluff stats, emotions **drive** decisions. Bold, authentic marketing builds trust by showing real values in action. As one chief marketing officer noted, **"Bold campaigns succeed when they align with brand values and feel genuine"**. In other words, playing a strong role (even a risky one) in culture can win love and loyalty.

In the CPG world, campaigns like Always #LikeAGirl or Pampers (when they do gut-punch ads) prove purpose-driven boldness sells. In tech, even B2B companies see the value: a recent survey warned that corporate ads need more humor and stories, not just specs. Fashion labels, by nature, **must** be bold: **Balenciaga's muddy catwalk**, **Gucci's surreal photo shoots**, or **Chanel's cinematic ads** thrive on going beyond the obvious. Nike's "Dream Crazy" fit that mold, too.

Bold isn't a naughty word; it's an **opportunity**. Your clients want their brand to be remembered, to be talked about, to matter. Mediocrity gets a yawn. The data scream it: **attention** is currency, and the only way to mint it at scale is to break molds.

So, go ahead, **sell that crazy idea**. Name it, package it, and champion it with confidence. Use a killer story, show them

the losses of doing nothing, drop in proof of peers succeed-
ing, and be honest about the risks. Trust yourself and the
stats: in today's shark-tank market, **bold moves win**. After
all, as Saul Colt would tell you (I sometimes speak in third
person like Rickey), sometimes the most creative thing you
can do is ignore the rulebook (just make sure you have a
better one to offer).

Stories can be fantastic; you might want to use them.
However, there's a 'but'… a story can limit our ability to
process facts. Wise words for any pitch: Use a story to
enchant, but back it up with facts so solid they scare even
your own heart.

And remember: your job isn't to talk them into a leap; it's
to calmly pull them to the ledge, spotlight the ocean below,
and show them why flying might just be better than
safe-falling.

9 /
flip, fly, or repeat: bouncing back when they say "no"

GETTING SHOT DOWN flat on your face sucks. (Science shows social rejection lights up your brain's pain center.) But that's biology, not destiny. Even the all-time greats got knocked down. What do they do? They hustle up, pivot, or laugh it off. You should too.

First, vent a bit. Shake your fist at the moon, compose an angry text (that you don't send), or smash a stress ball. Okay, now breathe. Time to play scientist: dissect the feedback calmly. Was it the timing? The tone? The missing data? No shame in asking "why not?" and using the answer. If you can tweak and re-pitch a sharper angle, do it. (Fun fact: Twitter started as a pivot after a podcasting project tanked.) If not, let it go and focus on a new idea.

ALWAYS REMEMBER: failure isn't a personality trait, it's data. Thomas Edison "failed" thousands of times testing lightbulb filaments, but he didn't call it failure , just finding ten thousand ways that won't work. Picasso had plenty of awful sketches. The only permanent failure is quitting.

. . .

RESILIENCE PRO TIPS:

Pro tip (Inspect, then pivot): Treat every "no" as free feedback. If it flopped, adapt or scrap it fast , rinse, repeat.

Pro tip (Reframe with a growth mindset): Don't let that "no" define you. It's one data point, not a prophecy. (Your brain may sting, but you can out-think it.)

Pro tip (Lean on allies): Don't sulk alone. Vent to a mentor or teammate briefly, then refocus. Creative work is a team sport.

Pro tip (Keep perspective): Most bold ideas fail (remember that 95% of launches flop). But every time you swing, you increase the odds of the next crazy thing working.

SHAKE IT OFF, fix what you can, and get back in the arena. Each rejection is just one draft away from a killer final campaign.

RECAP: We've covered how to sell fearless ideas to the skeptics, how to plan and execute them like a pro, and how to bounce back when you crash. Next up, we turn the lens on you. In the final chapters we'll show how all these wild adventures forge your personal brand and word-of-mouth legend. After all, surviving this rollercoaster is story gold , and the way you tell that story can make you unforgettable.

10 /
execute big, play smart: doing crazy without losing your mind

GOT THE GREEN LIGHT? Awesome. Now comes the grind, the planning and execution. Treat it like a military operation. Red Bull spent seven years prepping Stratos (with engineers, test jumps, and countless checklists). Map every step, assign owners for each task, and assume something will go wrong. Pro Tip: Use checklists like a pilot. (If NASA engineers needed them for moonshots, you need them for a stunt.)

EXPECT CHAOS. Stuff will break: printers jam, weather shifts, interns faint. Keep your team's cool. Assign a "devil's advocate" to spot risks early and a "project captain" who solves fires on the fly. Communicate constantly, daily huddles, shared docs, instant alerts. KFC's Mojave Desert logo used 65,000 tiles, so they locked down permits and logistics before launch. They even planned PR for sneaking Sanders into the UN. Learn from that: always have legal and PR on standby.

Pro Tip: Pack redundancies. Extra batteries, backup laptops, backup ideas, treat Plan B like Plan A's twin. If your stunt involves fire or flying, hire pros to stand by. In short: play the whole game, not just the highlight reel. Build in fallbacks so the audience sees the fun even if Plan A sputters.

FAIL LIKE A BOSS: Bouncing Back When Your Campaign Flops

I have never had a failed project but I understand it happens to some people and if your wild idea tanked. Brush it off, you're in good company. Roughly 95% of new products or big launches fail, so this is normal. Thomas Edison didn't curse after 9,000 broken filaments; he quipped "I now know definitely over 9,000 ways an electric light bulb will not work.". Take a page from creative champs: Picasso once burned bad sketches to keep warm, "Every act of creation is first an act of destruction.". Oprah's OWN network was mocked as a flop, but she remembered "Trouble don't last always" and turned it around. This mindset, resilience, is literally "the capacity to bounce back".

Pro Tip: Practice rejection therapy. Make "no" boring by self-inflicted exposure. Email a celeb asking for a ludicrous favor (I do this a lot and is the main reason B0bcat Goldthwait may have a restraining order on me) or cold-call an ex for a meeting, just to train your ears to rejection. Psychologists find that repeated "no" turns the sting into just another data point. After a few fake "nos", an actual exec rejection will feel like a shrug. You'll develop a, "Well, that stung a bit, what's next?" attitude.

DEBRIEF LOGICALLY. What happened vs. what you expected? Maybe your message confused people, or the timing was off. Use it as data. Pivot your idea: learn from Dyson, who needed 5,127 prototypes to perfect his vacuum. If part of your stunt can be salvaged, grab it! Reframe "we wasted X" into "we earned Y insight." The bombed campaign is just homework for the next try. Keep iterating. (I sometimes joke, "At least no one threw a live chicken at me yet," just to break the tension.)

PRO TIPS at a Glance

Pitching: Sell the fear of missing out, not just upside. Cite big-brand wins (social proof) and losses avoided (loss aversion).

Execution: Plan the stunt like a mission, assign clear roles, build redundancies, and over-communicate every step. Keep the core fun concept alive; cut anything that dilutes the magic.

Bounce-Back: Keep a growth mindset. Treat each flop as research. As Edison said, "I have not failed... I've just found thousands of ways that won't work." Every setback is just the next plot twist.

Remember: you're playing the long game. Those banana stands and chicken corsages will be legendary case studies. Red Bull's space jump? Iconic. Your bombed idea? Just an epic war story waiting to be told, as long as you get back up. Ballsy marketing is high-risk, high-reward (and way more fun). Now go pitch like your career depends on it (because it does).

EXECUTE BIG, Play Smart

Big stunts are part blockbuster and part logistics. Think of Red Bull's Stratos jump or KFC's giant Colonel face in the Nevada desert, these weren't throwaway promos, they were epic productions. Red Bull's 2012 space jump, for example, was "not just a stunt; it was a masterclass in branding, innovation, and the power of social media". The team literally treated it like a NASA mission: they spent years planning every detail. In fact, Red Bull "meticulously planned" Stratos over several years with scientists, engineers and even former astronaut Joe Kittinger to design Felix Baumgartner's capsule and pressure suit. (Every engineer and welder became a co-creator.) KFC's so-called "spacevertisement" was equally ambitious: it had about 50 designers and craftspeople spend three months laying out 65,000 painted tiles in the desert to create Sanders's face, a billboard so huge it was visible from orbit. These examples show that **execution is itself a creative act**: each logistic move, from drawing up the capsule blueprints to placing every tile in the sand, was part of the stunt's story, not an afterthought.

Pro Tip:
    Build a long runway. Work backwards from your go-live date. As Red Bull and KFC prove, these stunts

often require months or years of prep. Create a time-line like a launch schedule, allowing time for design, testing, permits and approvals.

COORDINATE Your Crew

A huge stunt needs a well-oiled crew. This means dozens (or even hundreds) of people working in concert, much like a movie production. Red Bull's Stratos mission had a NASA-style "mission control" setup, with engineers, doctors and specialists in constant contact with Baumgartner's team. WestJet's 2013 Christmas Miracle turned the airline's own employees into actors: Producer Kegan Sant reports that they filmed in both Toronto and Calgary over 7 hours, with "teams on the ground in both cities" and real-time coordination to get each traveler's wish. Every gift request was relayed from Blue Santa's digital screen in Toronto to shoppers and bag handlers in Calgary. Even the smallest staffers became part of the plot, WestJet gave each of its 12,000 employees a "Blue Santa" hat and a mini-budget for random acts of holiday kindness. Suddenly gate agents and baggage crews were key players in the narrative.

Pro Tip:

Give everyone a role. Align internal teams early so every person understands the vision. WestJet's campaign literally turned its staff into street performers and surprise-gifters. Set up a "mission command" (even a simple group chat or dashboard) to keep teammates synced across locations.

Pro Tip:

Appoint a director and a producer. Assign clear leaders for creative direction and for logistics. On set, the producer (like Kegan Sant on WestJet's shoot) will "never sugar coat a problem" but will solve it on the fly. Make sure everyone from PR to safety has a point person.

PLAN for (and Mitigate) Risks

Big stunts have big risk. From weather to technical failure to legal headaches, you need Plan B (and C…) for anything that could go wrong. Red Bull learned this the hard way: a 2008 court injunction over the balloon system pushed the jump back years. The team even had to address uncharted physiological concerns about breaking the sound barrier in freefall. In execution, they built multiple safety layers: Baumgartner's suit had redundant life-support systems, and he had a backup parachute in case of blackout. They also identified the riskiest moments in advance. For example, the first 3,000 feet of balloon ascent was known to the team as "the death maneuver", fragile airbag material and a sudden wind could tear it, so 18–20 technicians were on deck just to steer the balloon gently during that phase.

Pro Tip:

Rehearse like it's real. Treat your stunt like a live mission. Practice each step under pressure, ideally in full costume or environment. As one WestJet producer said of their real-time airport shoot, "you couldn't afford to make a mistake", the pressure was very real. This means doing dry-runs of the reveal, the camera angles, and even failure modes.

Pro Tip:

Inventory the what-ifs. List your biggest "bad outcomes" (e.g. gift truck stuck in traffic, balloon leak, internet cutout) and assign backups. Bring spare parts, extra batteries, substitute presenters or props. WestJet, for example, had backup gifts ready if any passengers' presents didn't arrive on time. And always have safety and insurance in place, none of these stunts are worth it if someone gets hurt or you wake up to a PR disaster.

Pro Tip:

Check regulations. I don't do this but for you to not end up in jail you should not ignore things like permits or legal issues. Red Bull had to lobby for years and file paperwork with aviation authorities before Stratos was "go." Factor in time for city permits, FAA/transport approvals, and privacy releases. A stunt that flies under the radar can get grounded if you're not compliant.

MAKE Execution Part of the Show

Remember: the way you stage the stunt is **itself** a creative expression. Design every detail to be "Instagrammable" and on-brand. Red Bull didn't just send Felix into space; they framed the scene for maximum drama, from the giant helium balloon rising at dawn to the live TV countdown and the look of Baumgartner's red-white-blue suit. In WestJet's case, Santa's check-in kiosk was custom-built, Blue Santa's speech on the digital screen was charmingly scripted, and camera crews were hidden to capture genuine surprise. Producer

Kegan Sant noted that their Christmas shoot "pioneered a genre" of using real people in a commercial; it involved "multiple cameras, wireless connectivity and real time monitoring" that "had never been done for commercials" before. Every lighting cue, camera angle and sound effect was intentionally orchestrated to pull on heartstrings. Even KFC hid a mini-game in its stunt, the Colonel's tie tiles contained the hidden message "FINGER LICKIN' GOOD," and 10,000-$1 coupons were awarded to fans who spotted it. That Easter egg turned a giant brand logo into an interactive treasure hunt.

Pro Tip:

Think in scenes and shots. Storyboard the event. What is the final frame or headline moment? WestJet planned for the luggage carousel reveal and the family reactions; KFC made sure satellites and Google Earth cameras could see their logo. Use visuals (lighting, props, color) that echo your brand.

Pro Tip:

Stay on message. Tie everything back to your core value. Red Bull's "give you wings" mantra was literally realized by sending a man sky-high. WestJet's spirit of caring shone through in the Santa setup and gift-giving. Keep logos and taglines visible (even subtly) so people connect the stunt to your brand.

Pro Tip:

Engage the audience. Give viewers a way in. Use hashtags or challenges. Red Bull harnessed #RedBull-Stratos to trend globally. WestJet used #WestJet-Christmas to collect user videos. Little touches

(contests, photo ops, souvenirs) make your stunt share-able content, not just an isolated happening.

AMPLIFY AND EXTEND the Magic

The stunt doesn't end when the ribbon is cut or the balloon lands. In fact, that's just the launchpad. Plan a post-event campaign to ride the wave of attention. Red Bull relentlessly recycled Stratos footage, they streamed Felix's jump live to a record 9.5 million concurrent viewers, then followed up with highlight reels and documentaries to keep the buzz going. WestJet released its Christmas video immediately, and it **took off**: over 40 million views in the first month. News outlets worldwide played clips, and even the CBC did a 10-minute feature. The team invited press on a "Blue Santa" flight across the country and toured morning shows so every media rail talked about it. By inviting journalists and influencers into the process, they turned the stunt itself into a story.

Pro Tip:

Lock in media partners ahead of time. Let key journalists or influencers in on the secret early. WestJet flew reporters on location and gave them interviews with Santa, so the news cycle was primed as the stunt went live.

Pro Tip:

Prep content for every channel. Have your videos, blog posts and press releases ready to drop. Tease clips beforehand to build hype (as Red Bull did), then release the full video at peak moment. Post-stunt, publish behind-the-scenes footage and follow-up stories (which WestJet's blog used to rack up 700K page views).

Pro Tip:

Measure and celebrate. Track your hashtags, views and media mentions. Compile the metrics and positive feedback (WestJet tallied millions of social impressions and a $2.26M earned-media value) to justify the effort. And most importantly, learn what resonated so you can scale it next time.

TREATING execution as creative itself means every bolt, gift, and camera angle is intentional. The best big-brand stunts prove that when you synchronize creative vision with military-precision planning, you generate moments people will **share** and remember. Start with a bold idea, then play it smart: build the right team, rehearse relentlessly, mitigate risks, and plan to **tell** the story before, during, and after. With that mindset, and the pro tips above, even the wildest experiential campaign can land safely on its feet, excite audiences, and amplify your brand without compromising safety or message.

11 /
word of mouth marketing: how to make everyone talk (and laugh, think, cry)

IF THIS BOOK does well my next one will go very deep on Word Of Mouth Marketing...but incase this book doesn't do well I'll share a little of what I know now so there because, well, most of the ideas and concepts I have shared or dreamed up are textbook, *or whatever this book is*, examples of strategic Word Of Mouth Marketing.

WHY AM I such a loudmouth about word of mouth? Because it flat-out works. People have been recommending products they love (and warning friends about the duds) since the invention of, well, people. It's marketing at its most human and basic: person to person, trust by association. In an age where consumers have trust issues with advertising, a friend's recommendation is like gold wrapped in bacon, or fresh Cholent for my jewish readers, basically irresistible.

DON'T TAKE my word for it; take Nielsen's.

> In a global survey, 92% of consumers said they trust recommendations from people they know over all other forms of advertising.

Compare that to the trust in traditional ads (hovering in the ballpark of 40-50% for most paid media) and you see why WOM packs a punch. In fact, personal referrals are consistently rated the most trustworthy source of brand information.

IT'S NOT JUST TRUST in an abstract sense, word of mouth drives real, tangible results. A landmark study sponsored by the Word of Mouth Marketing Association (WOMMA) found that WOM drives about 13% of consumer sales, equating to roughly $6 trillion in annual spending. You read that right: trillions with a "T," all stirred up by conversations over coffee, tweets, DMs, and yes, mostly face-to-face chats (remember those?). And here's the kicker: WOM doesn't just create new sales on its own; it makes your other marketing work harder. The WOMMA study showed that word of mouth has a powerful amplifying effect on paid media, boosting the results of ad campaigns by as much as 15%. It's the rising tide that lifts all boats in your marketing harbor.

TRADITIONAL ADVERTISING, on the other hand, is facing an epidemic of tune-out. People are DVR-ing past commercials, installing ad-blockers, and developing laser-like banner blindness. We're conditioned to be skeptical of anything with a whiff of corporate sell. Word of mouth flips that script. Instead of you bragging about your own product

("Of course you think your widget is world-changing; you made it!"), you get your customers to do the bragging for you. And when people brag about you, it doesn't sound like bragging, it sounds like truth. Real customers don't gain anything by singing a brand's praises (aside from maybe the warm glow of recommending something awesome), which is why their praise carries weight.

LET me give you a dramatic example. A while back, Nielsen also noted that 84% of consumers take action based on personal recommendations, meaning they don't just trust their friends, they buy because of them. Think about the last time a buddy or colleague raved, "You have to try this place, it's the best tacos in town." Odds are, you ended up at that taco joint within the week. (If you're like me, you not only went but you brought three friends.) Now contrast that with a billboard that screams "WE HAVE THE BEST TACOS!" in 10-foot letters. Maybe you notice it, maybe you don't. Maybe you believe it... but probably you roll your eyes, because every taco place says they're the best. The friend's recommendation wins every time, because it comes pre-loaded with credibility and social proof.

AND SPEAKING OF SOCIAL PROOF, let's talk about why that matters so much in WOM.

Trust in different forms of advertising: notice how "recommendations from people I know" tops the chart at 92%, leagues above any form of paid advertising. Word of mouth turns your customers into your most trusted ad channel.

THE SIMPLE TRUTH IS THIS: People trust people more than they trust ads. Word of mouth marketing harnesses that truth and puts it to work for your brand. Instead of pouring another dollar into interrupting people who are actively ignoring you (hello, 5-second skip on YouTube ads), WOM invites your customers to spread the word voluntarily, enthusiastically, and often unpredictably. That unpredictability is a bit scary, you can't script word of mouth the way you script a TV spot, but it's also what makes it authentic. And authenticity is in short supply in marketing. When your brand does something talk-worthy, your audience amplifies it for you. They become your marketing department (and I promise their salary requirements are very reasonable, most will work for free, or maybe for the occasional free swag or heartfelt thank-you).

TO SUM IT UP: WOM works because it earns attention and trust, rather than trying to buy it. It's fundamentally more persuasive. Don't get me wrong, I'm not saying to fire your media buying team and set your billboard budget on fire (though that would be a hell of a stunt...). Traditional advertising has its place for reach and awareness. But if you want conviction, if you want customers who are downright evangelical about your brand, word of mouth is the spark you need. It's the difference between hearing about a brand and believing in a brand.

THE CORE PRINCIPLES OF WOM: How to Generate Buzz on Purpose

So how do you actually get people talking? Contrary to popular belief, it's not luck, and it's not reserved for the Apples and Nikes of the world. There are some clear principles of WOM that anyone can apply, whether you're a scrappy startup, a local mom-and-pop, or, like some of my clients, a big company that wants to feel small again. Here are the core ideas I swear by:

Be Remarkable: Literally. Marketing know it all, Seth Godin said it years ago about products, and it holds true for marketing campaigns: Be remarkable (as in, worth making a remark about). If you want word of mouth, you have to do or offer something that jolts people out of their apathy. That could mean hilariously creative, shocking (in a good way), heartwarming, or just plain different. My personal approach is using humor and surprise, I love making people laugh because laughter breaks down barriers. But "remarkable" could also be an exceptional customer service gesture or a bold stance on an issue (more on that later). The litmus test is simple: Would someone tell a friend about this? If not, back to the drawing board. In my FreshBooks days, for example, we made our customer appreciation so over-the-top that it became a talking point (I once sent flowers on behalf of Fresh-Books to a woman who got stood up on a date, just to brighten her day. You better believe she told people about that kind of unexpected kindness and we even got media attention..but that wasn't why I did it).

TAP INTO EMOTIONS (LAUGH, Think, or Cry). Here's my famous Laugh/Think/Cry filter: I aim for every campaign or stunt to make people laugh, think, or cry. Preferably laugh (I'm a sucker for fun), but any strong emotion will do. Why? Because emotion = motivation. When you strike an emotional chord, people not only remember, they share. Think about the content you yourself share on social media, it's the stuff that made you crack up, or touched your heart, or blew your mind with insight. Bland doesn't get shared. As I often say, if you don't cross that line, you're not making memories; you're not creating conversations. Being safe is the riskiest strategy of all, because nobody talks about the brand that politely stayed in its comfort zone. If you want proof, look at any guerrilla marketing win, it's always a bit audacious. When we (re) launched Xero (cloud accounting software) in the U.S., I leaned into stunt marketing that made accountants, a typically stoic bunch, actually laugh and have fun. (Picture me re-enacting Evel Knievel's motorcycle jump over school buses while shouting, "Online Invoicing: So easy, it's a leap you can handle!", accountants still mention that ridiculous visual years later.) The point is, stir feelings, and you'll stir up conversations.

MAKE IT ABOUT THEM, not you. This is huge. So many brands forget that the customer is the hero of the story. If your marketing is all "me, me, me," why would anyone feel compelled to repeat it? But if you shine the spotlight on your customers, they'll step into it and own the narrative, and their friends will listen. I call this building customer parades. Case in point: at a big tech conference, my team and I once quite literally turned our users into celebrities for a day.

We organized a "FreshBooks Customer Parade" at Collision Conference (in New Orleans) complete with an authentic New Orleans marching band and our logo'd banner, where our actual customers marched through the venue while we cheered them on. The ideas was since everyone was stuck in the conference centre we would bring a little of the city inside, we even gave out 2000 beignets. Was it slightly absurd? Absolutely. Did it draw a crowd? Heck yes. We treated our customers like rock stars; people snapped photos and videos (hello, shareable moment!), and the participants themselves couldn't stop talking about how a company actually celebrated them in public.

Similarly, at SXSW one year I was working with Rogers communications on a news service called Thoora. Instead of handing out lame flyers about our software, we printed a daily 4-page newspaper featuring the top news stories from the world and the event...and yes there was even original comic strips from things we overheard at the event. We would produce the paper at midnight every night and pick them up around 4am so we could do room drops at every hotel room in the downtown core. This stunt almost killed me from exhaustion but it was worth it when I heard people say "Have you seen these? This is so cool!", people were bragging about being in the paper and wondered how we put it together with almost real time information.

The result: Thoora wasn't just another vendor at the conference; we were the company inside the conference. That's WOM gold. The lesson: if you make your customers feel like the star of the show, they'll happily tell everyone about the experience.

Social Proof is Your Secret Sauce. People are social creatures; if we see a crowd, we instinctively think, "What's the fuss about? Maybe I should check it out." WOM leverages this psychology at every turn. Testimonials, reviews, and public customer love are not vanity fluff, they're conversion fuel.

Data backs this up:

Almost 80% of consumers check ratings and reviews before making a purchase, and a vast majority trust online reviews as much as personal recommendations. That's right, even strangers' opinions on the internet can carry more weight than your polished ad copy.

Why? Because of perceived authenticity. So use that. Show off your five-star reviews, proudly share user-generated content, encourage customers to leave testimonials, and respond to them visibly. A positive review is two gifts in one: a piece of persuasive content and a signal to that customer's network that your brand is legit. Social proof also means highlighting engagement. If a lot of people are interacting with your product or your brand online, lean into it. On the flip side, if no one's talking about you on your channels, that silence is also noticed (and not great). So you might need to kickstart the conversation yourself (start a community, pose questions, feature customer stories regularly). Remember, everyone wants to join the party that everyone else seems to be enjoying. Part of my WOM strategy for any client is to engineer moments that are inherently shareable, what I call *"shareable moments"*. For example, we ran a campaign for an app launch where we set up a giant, bizarre vending machine in downtown Toronto that dispensed free goodies only if two people used the app together (we literally made people high-five and hit a giant button together). It created a spectacle, crowds form, phones come out, social media lights up with pictures of this wacky machine and the smiling people who just scored free swag by cooperating. That visible excitement is infectious. As more folks gathered, even the skeptics on the fringe thought, "Hmm, I don't want to miss out." That's social proof in action: seeing others engage and enjoy convinces new folks to give it a try.

GIVE THEM A STORY TO TELL. Ultimately, WOM is about storytelling. People don't share "marketing campaigns," they share stories and experiences. So give them a damn good story. This might mean doing something unexpected or outrageous that naturally turns into a story. When I launched Zipcar in Canada, the company expected me to throw a modest little party for our early members, something normal and forgettable. Nope, not my style. Instead, I took the tiny budget and threw a rock concert for all our members. (this story again?) I begged, borrowed, and bartered to make it happen, trading free Zipcar rides to bands in exchange for them playing, partnering with a local venue, getting a co-sponsor to chip in. The result: we packed the place with customers rocking out together, having an absolute blast because of our brand. It cost peanuts, but the impact was huge. People talked about "that time Zipcar threw a killer concert" for years. It became part of Zipcar's lore in Toronto. That's what you want, a narrative that customers latch onto and propagate. Another example: We once noticed a Major League Baseball team (go Blue Jays!) wasn't selling out certain sections of their stadium. Instead of seeing empty seats, I saw an opportunity. We partnered with the team to fill an empty section with hundreds of our clients and prospects, basically a massive FreshBooks fan outing at the ballpark. We turned it into an event-within-an-event: custom T-shirts, shout-outs on the jumbotron, and a post-game happy hour. To everyone else at the game, it looked like FreshBooks had taken over (social proof!), and to those in our crowd, it felt like being part of an exclusive club. Afterward, you can bet those attendees had stories: "I got to sit in a special Fresh-Books section at the game, it was awesome!" and even fans nearby were curious who this enthusiastic group was. The story spread, and FreshBooks earned a rep as that cool company that does fun, unexpected stuff for its customers. Give people an anecdote that makes them look interesting when they retell it, and they will retell it. It's human nature, we all want to have the best story at dinner.

The Zipcar New Music Experience Party

The Phoenix Concert Theatre in Toronto – Galaxy live concert at Zipcar Party.

Trust Your Customers (and earn their trust). WOM is a two-way street built on trust. You have to trust your customers, trust them with your brand message out in the wild, and in turn, do everything to earn and keep their trust. That means your product or service has to deliver (no amount of buzz will save a crappy product in the long run, because people will figure it out and then they'll talk, but for the wrong reasons). It also means being transparent, honest, and responsive. If a customer says something about your brand, good or bad, acknowledge it. Thank them for the praise or address the criticism. People watch how brands handle feedback.

Fun fact: 80% of consumers say they trust a brand more when it actively responds to and engages with reviews, even negative ones. Ignoring customers (or worse, censoring them) is a trust-killer. But handling feedback with grace can turn a skeptic into a believer, and it shows onlookers that you're a company that cares. I've gotten more WOM mileage out of good customer service moments than any ad campaign could dream of. Each one is an investment in goodwill that pays off when those customers tell their friends, "Yeah, there was an issue, but they were so great about fixing it."

THESE PRINCIPLES all interconnect and feed each other. Be remarkable and emotional, and you give them a story. Make it about them and use social proof, and you amplify the story. Trust them and they'll trust you, fueling even more recommendations. It's a virtuous cycle of chatter.

SOCIAL PROOF: The Fuel that Keeps WOM Running

Let's drill a bit deeper into social proof, because it's the linchpin of so much of this. Social proof is a fancy term for a simple phenomenon: people follow the lead of others. Especially in situations where they're not sure what to do or whom to trust, they look around and take cues. In marketing, social proof can take many forms, reviews, testimonials, case studies, influencer endorsements, user counts ("Join the 50,000 people who've already downloaded!"), social media engagement numbers, you name it. In WOM, social proof isn't just a byproduct; it's a strategy. We consciously create conditions to showcase or simulate the crowd consensus in our favor.

WHY IS IT SO IMPORTANT? Because nobody wants to be the sucker. It's harsh but true. If I'm considering buying a product and I see a bunch of other savvy people I respect saying it's great, I feel safer pulling the trigger. Conversely, if I hear crickets, or worse, hear negative buzz, I'll pause. Marketers have known this forever, which is why you see things like "best-selling" on book covers or laugh tracks in sitcoms (to cue you that other people found it funny, so maybe you should too). But in the era of consumer empower-ment, the authenticity of social proof matters more than ever. Consumers are cynical about brands tooting their own horn ("#1 in customer satisfaction!* (***according to our own survey**)"). They put more stock in user-generated proof.

CONSIDER THIS: 75% of consumers report looking for reviews and testimonials before buying something. And 72% say positive testimonials make them trust a business more. That's huge. It means before a potential customer even thinks about giving you money, they're hunting for signs that other real people have had a good experience. I've had clients come to me perplexed that their fancy ad campaign isn't convert-ing, and the first thing I'll check is their reviews or social pres-ence. If those are barren or bad, no slick advertisement will overcome that deficit of trust. Social proof is the context that makes all your other marketing either believable or BS.

SO HOW DO you leverage social proof in WOM? Here are a few actionable ways (learned the fun way, through trial, error, and the occasional facepalm moment): Cultivate and high-light testimonials. Don't wait for happy customers to magi-cally decide to write glowing paragraphs about you, ask them! The moment you hear a customer say, "I love what you guys do," swoop in like an over-caffeinated journalist: "That's amazing, would you be willing to put that in writing? We'd love to feature your experience." Most happy customers are happy to oblige. Then you showcase those testimonials every-where appropriate, your website, your deck, social media, even in-store if you have a physical location (you know those walls at some restaurants plastered with customer Polaroids and comments? That's social proof in analog form). A well-crafted testimonial from someone who resembles your target audience is marketing gold. It's essentially word of mouth on the record.

ENCOURAGE reviews (and don't fear the bad ones). A lot of businesses are scared of asking for reviews because, gasp, what if someone says something negative? Here's the reality: A negative review here or there can actually enhance credibility, it proves you're not airbrushing the truth. People tend to be skeptical if a product has only five-star reviews; it seems too good to be true (and maybe fake). According to one study,

when brands only show perfect 5-star reviews, it actually reduces trust for many consumers.

So embrace a bit of imperfection. Ideally, you respond to any less-than-stellar reviews with understanding and a genuine willingness to make it right. That response itself is social proof that you care (and as noted, the vast majority of customers appreciate when brands address issues and will trust you more for it).

SHOW VISIBLE CUSTOMER ENGAGEMENT. This can mean different things depending on your business. It might be social media interactions ("Look, people are actually commenting on and sharing our posts!"), or forum discussions about your product, or lines out the door of your shop. One tactic I've used is what I call the customer spotlight: regularly feature a customer on your channels, not just as a testimonial, but as a story. It not only flatters that customer (who then shares it with their friends, generating, you guessed it, more word of mouth), but it signals to everyone watching that people use and love your product enough to be showcased. It turns your marketing from a monologue into a dialogue, where customers have a voice. That's powerful. It subtly tells a prospect, "People like you are part of this brand's story. If you join us, you'll be celebrated too." That feeling of inclusion can tip someone from considering to converting.

ENGINEER SHAREABLE MOMENTS. I touched on this earlier, but it's worth reiterating: try to create moments in your customer experience that are so delightful or novel that people can't help but share them. Think unboxing experiences that are Instagram-worthy (I once sent a small box of cereal with a "prize inside" every package we shipped, customers started posting pics and thank you's with unsolicited reviews and love.

Or an in-app Easter egg that users stumble on and tweet about. Or an event that's visually striking (ever see those pop-up museums where every room is an elaborate selfie back-drop? Those are basically WOM factories). The idea is to bake marketing into your product or campaign such that the use or experience of it inherently generates content for the user to share. When people share those moments, each post is social proof to others: "hey, this looks fun / valuable / popular."

LEVERAGE INFLUENCER SOCIAL PROOF CAREFULLY.

You might be thinking, "Isn't influencer marketing basically paid word of mouth?" In a sense, yes, you're paying people to spread the word. But be careful: Today's audiences are extremely savvy. They know an #ad when they see one, and big follower counts don't impress like they used to. In fact, a lot of traditional influencer posts scream "inauthentic" and don't move the needle on trust. As I've argued often, most influencers do not actually influence sales.

This goes back to KLT - Know/Like/Trust. You may know and like the influencer but deep down you know they are getting paid to say nice things so can you really trust them?

Followers might "like" a post of theirs, but that doesn't mean they run out and buy the product. I'm far more interested in micro-influencers and genuine fans. A micro-influencer (say someone with 500 or 5,000 followers who is truly passionate about your niche) can have disproportionately big impact because their audience actually trusts their opinions. They're essentially regular people with louder voices. When they recommend something, it feels real (because it often is). For example, for a food brand client, instead of blowing the budget on a celebrity chef who'd half-heartedly post once, we engaged 20 local food bloggers and Instagram foodies who already loved the product. We just gave them more reason and material to talk about it (exclusive recipes, behind-the-scenes visits, etc.).

THE RESULT WAS an avalanche of authentic content and endorsements. Each of those was social proof to a tight-knit audience. So yes, use influencers, but use the right ones and let them speak in their own voice. And always prioritize the organic advocates you already have. They are the ones who will stick around and keep talking because they actually like you, not because you cut a check.

SOCIAL PROOF IS both an outcome of successful WOM and an input that makes future WOM easier. Once you have momentum, people talking about you, leaving good reviews, sharing experiences, you've got proof that others can see and join. Your job is to keep that flywheel spinning: keep delivering share-worthy experiences, keep engaging your community, and keep showcasing the love you receive to inspire more.

MY PLAYBOOK…AND Other WOM Secrets

Every word of mouth marketer develops their own bag of tricks over time, little tactics or philosophies that consistently work. I've already let you in on a few of mine (hey, I'm feeling generous, and you bought the book, so you deserve the good stuff). But let's put them in one place and add a couple more. Think of this as Saul's WOM Playbook, distilled from a career of doing sometimes crazy, always interesting things to get brands talked about:

. . .

THE LAUGH/THINK/CRY Filter: Worth repeating (over and over over and over cause it works and it is all I got) because it's that important to my process. When brainstorming any campaign or stunt, I literally have a checklist in my head: will this make people laugh? Will it make them think "hmm that's clever" or "that's deep"? Will it touch an emotional nerve enough to mist up an eye? If I can't answer yes to at least one of those, the idea isn't strong enough. If I can hit two or three in one go, we're entering legendary territory. For example, a campaign we did for a real estate search engine called Zoocasa ticked all three boxes, it made people laugh, think and cry. The ideas was simple, to promote this real estate search engine we announced we launched and that we had an exclusive listing to sell The Rogers Centre (the baseball stadium of the Toronto Blue Jays). Since Zoocasa was owned by Rogers we got actual permission and created a really bad (on purpose) real estate video commenting on the 400 foot ceilings and 900 bathrooms. There was a lot of media and even a for sale sign in the lawn outside. We hosted a brokers open house and a public open house letting people see parts of the building they have never seen before. Those folks told everyone about that experience, it moved them. Emotion creates memory, and memory yields conversation. That's the goal of the filter.

The "Would I Tell My Friends?" Test: This one's simple. I put myself in the customer's shoes and ask, if I experienced this, would I be excited enough to tell my friends about it? It's amazing how many marketing ideas fail this test. A lot of marketing is, frankly, boring. If you wouldn't excitedly blab about your own campaign at a party, why the heck would anyone else? I have killed many a dull idea in the meeting room by asking this question. (Sometimes I phrase it more Saul-ish: "Guys, would anyone give a shit about this? No? Didn't think so. Next idea.") Be brutally honest with yourself here. "Interesting enough" is the bar. Always aim higher than the other brands in your space, remember, if your marketing looks like your competitor's, it isn't worth talking about.

CUSTOMER PARADES & **Hero-Making**: I shared how we did literal parades and baseball cards for customers. The broader philosophy is something I live by: make your customers look and feel awesome, and they'll do your marketing for you. This goes beyond events. It could be as subtle as featuring user success stories on your blog, not stories about how they use your product, but about them, their business, their life, with your brand just playing a supporting role. Or giving your top users a platform - e.g., invite them to co-create content, be on your podcast, takeover your Instagram for a day, etc.

At FreshBooks we had something we nicknamed the "Customer Hall of Fame", an informal program where we'd periodically send gifts or spotlights to customers who achieved milestones (like their millionth invoice sent through our system) or who were just super-engaged community members. These people became evangelists. They'd brag, "FreshBooks sent me a custom jersey when I hit a big billing milestone!" or "They featured my business in their news-letter!" That bragging is beautiful music to a WOM strategist's ears. When customers brag about being associated with you, you've hit WOM nirvana. It's no longer you tooting your horn; it's them proudly tooting it for you.

GET **People to Brag (Humblebrag counts too)**: This is related but worth its own highlight. A lot of word of mouth is essentially people bragging about their good taste or good fortune. "Oh, you haven't tried that app? I've been using it for months, it's great, let me show you." That statement translates to, "I'm in the know, I have great taste, and I'll graciously share this tip with you." We humans are funny creatures, even our altruistic sharing of recommendations has an ego element. So tap into that ego (benevolently, of course). How do you do that? By making your product, service, or marketing imply a status boost. Invite people to an exclusive beta so they feel special and talk about being one of the first.

CREATE a VIP referral program where if they refer 3 friends they get a title or badge (and they'll proudly say, "I'm an Ambassador for X"). Limited-edition merch for your brand can work too, if someone's wearing your cool T-shirt around town, they're a walking conversation starter ("Hey, you use FreshBooks too? Nice shirt!", true story: our FreshBooks shirts became so hip in the Toronto startup scene that people begged for them. Wearing one kind of signaled you were part of the club). One of my favorite examples: when Gmail launched in 2004, it was invite-only and scarce. People who snagged an account early were practically bragging, "I have Gmail", they gave it social currency. We crave things that make us look good to others. Align your WOM tactics with that craving.

· · ·

BUSINESS COURAGE (DON'T BE Boring): I preach what I call business courage. It means being willing to stick your neck out with unusual ideas and not freaking out at the first raised eyebrow in the boardroom. Let's be real: safe marketing is invisible. The world does not need another bland banner ad or another polite press release that nobody reads. Sometimes you have to be a bit bold, even controversial (when it fits your brand) to get noticed and talked about. Now, I'm not saying be outrageous for the sake of it, it has to tie back to your brand purpose or message in a clever way. But have the courage to zig when others zag. I've done stunts that made executives nervous, driving an SUV across the country to meet with hundreds of customers (This was different than the RV trip. This time we made 50 custom brand videos for customers of Hubba.com and we called it Hubba Across America), or my infamous campaign at Fresh-Books where I posted a cheeky Craigslist ad challenging QuickBooks (our giant competitor) to a user satisfaction showdown. Legal and PR had a minor heart attack, but guess what? It got tons of word of mouth and media coverage because it was gutsy and fun. We backed up our talk and it paid off. When you take a stand or do something ballsy, you give your fans ammunition to passionately defend and promote you. They'll say "This company isn't like the others, they have guts and personality!" That differentiation is priceless. In a world where so many brands play it safe, a bit of calculated risk is the safe path to being noticed. Or as I often bluntly put it:

"If you're not willing to piss someone off, you probably won't impress anyone."

Listen and Iterate (Crowdsource Your WOM): Here's one

you might not expect in a chapter about spreading the word: **_shut up and listen._** Some of the best WOM ideas I've executed came from listening to customers. Pay attention to what jokes or references your customers make about your brand. Pay attention to how they use your product in ways you didn't expect (that's how "life hacks" become marketing campaigns). For example, one of our Zipcar members in Toronto offhandedly said in a forum, "Zipcar is like having a friend who loans you their car whenever." My team saw that and thought, that's a pretty darn good way to describe it. We turned that into a campaign theme ("Friends with Cars - Join Zipcar") which members then picked up and repeated. Customers will often give you the social proof language or the story angle if you're listening. Also, if you have a community (online or offline), observe what topics get them excited, what content they share among themselves. Then feed more of that. WOM isn't purely top-down, it's a conversation. And conversations have at least as much listening as talking. The bonus is, when customers see you actually implement an idea or respond to feedback, they'll talk about that too: "Wow, this company really listens to us!" (Cue more trust, more loyalty, more positive chatter).

THAT'S a good chunk of the playbook, and I could keep going (I have strong opinions on everything from how to properly run a contest that people share, to why surprise giveaways beat loyalty cards). But these are the biggies. Keep these in your back pocket and you'll already be ahead of 90% of marketers out there still scratching their heads wondering why nobody tweets about their latest bland campaign.

WORD OF MOUTH vs. Traditional Advertising: When WOM Wins

Let's address the elephant in the room: Where does WOM fit in vis-à-vis traditional advertising? Do you do both? Ditch one for the other? Is WOM just a supplement or can it carry a campaign on its own? Having played in both sandboxes, here's my take, straight up.

TRADITIONAL ADVERTISING (THINK TV COMMERCIALS, print ads, paid digital ads, etc.) is great for reach and frequency. You want to blast a new product launch to millions overnight? Ads will do that… if you have the budget. But the thing is, traditional ads are all "push", you pushing your message onto the audience, and today's consumers have gotten really good at pushing back (or tuning out). Ads shout, "HEY LOOK AT ME!" and people are like, "Nah, I'm good." Meanwhile, WOM is more of a nudge from the side: "Psst, check this out, it's cool," and it comes from a friend or an organic experience, so your guard isn't up. It's pull vs. push. WOM pulls people in by piquing their curiosity or earning their trust, rather than bombarding them.

Now, WOM shines brightest in certain scenarios:

When trust is paramount. Launching a new brand and need to build credibility? WOM will give you that faster than any ad, because people hear about you from trusted sources (friends, peers, respected voices) from day one. In fact, 64% of marketers (in a WOMMA survey) said they find word-of-mouth more effective than traditional marketing for credibility and engagement.

WHEN BUDGETS ARE LEAN. I often joke that I got into WOM because I was never given a big budget to blow on fancy ads, so I had to get creative. But it's true: if you have champagne aspirations on a beer budget, WOM is your friend. Stunts, community building, referral programs, these can cost a fraction of a mass media buy and can sometimes have outsized impact. My Zipcar rock concert stunt, for example, cost maybe 5% of what a citywide billboard campaign would've, yet it generated press coverage, sign-ups, and enduring word of mouth that no billboard could match. Word of mouth campaigns often rely more on time, creativity, and boldness than cash. And once they get rolling, they have a self-sustaining quality (people keep sharing) whereas ads stop working the moment your spending stops.

WHEN DIFFERENTIATION IS NEEDED. If you're in a crowded market and everyone's advertising looks the same (looking at you, SaaS companies with your stock-photo smiling office workers...), WOM is how you break free from the pack. Do something nobody else has the guts to do. It's hard to differentiate in a 30-second ad when the format is rigid and everyone's using the same playbook ("Show product, list features, have happy customer testimonial, insert generic tagline"). But in WOM, you write your own rules, host an unconventional event, create a quirky persona for your brand that interacts personally with customers, whatever. The WOM approach inherently stands out because it's not confined to the template. When FreshBooks was up against 800-pound gorilla QuickBooks, we didn't try to outspend them in ads (impossible). We out-thought them with WOM and stunts.

NOW, **traditional advertising still has advantages**: control (you control the message fully, whereas WOM you only influence what others say) and scale on demand (you can reach a million people in a day if you have the money, whereas WOM might take time to ripple out). And I'm not here to trash all traditional advertising, a clever ad can still work, and advertising can reinforce the word of mouth by increasing brand visibility. But in terms of effectiveness per dollar and depth of impact, WOM often wins. A recommendation from a friend might reach fewer people at a time, but it goes deeper, it sticks, it convinces. An ad might wash over 100 people with a 1% conversion, whereas a personal referral might convert 20% or more of the 10 people who hear it. WOM is the scalpel to advertising's hammer.

The best strategy often marries the two: use advertising to prompt word of mouth or to support it. For example, you run a small targeted ad campaign not to drive direct sales, but to drive awareness of a contest or stunt you're doing, basically inviting people into the experience that will generate WOM. Or you do a big PR stunt (WOM) that gets tongues wagging, then follow up with retargeting ads to those who searched for you or visited your site during the buzz, capitalizing on the interest sparked by WOM. It doesn't have to be either/or. But if I had to pick where to invest for a brand that wants passionate customers and longevity, I'd pick community and conversation over commercials almost every time.

ONE MORE THING **on when WOM is more effective**: when your product is good. Sounds obvious, but it must be said, WOM will amplify whatever's true about your product. If it's great, people will share great experiences. If it's crap, word will get out even faster. Traditional advertising can sometimes sell a bad product for a while (by basically lying or glossing over reality) until the truth catches up. But WOM is a truth-teller from day one. So I advise: before you try to make people talk, make sure you've built something worth talking about. No marketing, WOM or otherwise, can save a dumpster fire. But if you have got something special, even if it's just special to a niche audience, WOM is how you fan those embers into a blaze.

12 /
actionable takeaways and final thoughts

WE'VE COVERED A LOT, and I've had a blast sharing these stories (even repeating a few) and strategies in my own irreverent way. But I want to leave you with some actionable takeaways, concrete things you can do to start building a brand that people can't shut up about:

Identify your talk triggers (Thanks Jay Baer): Ask yourself, what is truly noteworthy about my product or brand? If nothing, create something. Add an unexpected feature, craft an unusual customer policy, or do a one-off stunt that ties to your brand story. Give people an excuse to bring you up in conversation.

Invest in customer experience: The best WOM is a byproduct of an awesome customer experience. Map out your customer's journey and find opportunities to wow them (remember the flower-sending, the personal touches, the little extras). One "wow" moment can equal dozens of referrals. As the saying goes, under-promise and over-deliver, and your customers will do the selling.

Leverage your existing fans: Who are your happiest customers right now? Treat them like VIPs. Literally ask them to spread the word, you'd be surprised how willing people are to recommend you if you just nudge them and maybe sweeten the pot with a referral incentive. But also equip them: give them cool swag or content to share, or invite them to exclusive events. Turn fans into ambassadors.

Make it easy to share: Reduce friction in every way. Add share buttons, referral links, "tweet this" moments. If you have a physical presence, create Instagrammable spots (a funky mural with your hashtag, etc.). If you have packaging, slip a couple of extra business cards or a fun note encouraging them to tell a friend if they loved it. Ask for the referral at the right time (usually right after a positive experience).

Monitor the conversation: Stay plugged in to what people are saying about you online (and offline, via your support channels or sales team intel). Jump into those conversations when appropriate, thank people for kind words, and address concerns or questions. Show that there's a human behind the brand who cares. People will talk more when they feel heard and connected.

Measure WOM (beyond vanity metrics): It's notoriously tricky to measure word of mouth perfectly (since private conversations aren't exactly trackable), but use proxies. Track referral traffic, use special promo codes for referral campaigns, measure changes in organic mention volume on social media, survey new customers ("How did you hear about us? Who referred you?"). The data can justify the effort. For instance, if you find 30% of new customers came from referrals, and those customers have a higher lifetime value, boom, you've got your business case for WOMM. Remember the earlier stat, 84% of consumers take action on personal recs, that action can be measured in your sales if you set up ways to capture it.

Be patient and consistent: Word of mouth is a long game. It's like planting seeds. Some sprout overnight (viral hits), but many take time to grow through consistent watering (i.e., consistently delightful experiences). Don't be discouraged if your first stunt doesn't make you a trending topic. Look at the trendline of your brand mentions and customer growth. WOMM can snowball and then sustain itself, but you have to push that snowball initially and keep it packing on more snow. Stay at it, keep delighting, keep experimenting with creative ideas. Momentum builds.

Finally, let me emphasize a mindset: Bold, genuine, and generous. Be bold in your marketing, have the guts to be different and a little risky (nobody talks about the timid brand). Be genuine, you can't fake caring about your customers, so actually care; be authentic in your voice, like I've been authentic (maybe a little too authentic at times, but hey that's my style) with you here. And be generous, with your time, attention, and value to customers. Give them stories, give them reasons to smile, give them exceptional service. That generosity comes back tenfold in word of mouth.

I've used these principles to help companies from one-man startups to Fortune 500 firms create movements of fans and advocates. I've seen an accountant software company (not exactly the sexiest sector) ignite such devotion that its users tattooed the logo on their bodies, willingly. I've seen a car-sharing service grow in a new country primarily on the strength of its community buzz. I've seen professional services firms (think really "boring" industries) break out of obscurity by embracing fun, WOM-worthy campaigns that got even cynical executives chatting like excited school kids. This stuff isn't magic, but it can sure feel magical when it works..._**and oh BTW, I have generated 1 billion dollars of revenue in my career for my clients.**_

Word of mouth marketing turns your customers into your salesforce, your storytellers, your tribe. It's marketing with soul. And the best part? It's a hell of a lot of fun, for them and for you. When you do WOM right, you're not beating people over the head with ads they don't want; you're creating moments and movements they actively want to be a part of. You're building not just a customer base, but a fan base.

So go on, give them something to talk about. Make them laugh, make them think, or make them cry, just make them feel something. Be bold enough to be remembered and caring enough to be trusted. Do that, and your customers will carry your story to places no advertising budget could ever reach. That, my friends, is the true billion-dollar secret of word of mouth marketing. Now you've got the playbook, I can't wait to hear your story of how people couldn't stop talking about your brand. Go make some noise.

Carry the Torch: Create the Unforgettable

So here we are, the final chapter. You and me, one last time. If you've made it this far, either you really like my jokes or you fell asleep around chapter 3 and I've been background noise ever since (hey, no judgment). But seriously, take a moment to appreciate this milestone. We've journeyed through wild ideas, audacious stunts, and creative frameworks together, and now it's time to bring it all home.

This chapter isn't just a conclusion; it's a commencement. Think of it as my personal send-off as you head out to wreak glorious havoc in the world of marketing (and beyond). By now, you're not just a reader, you're an accomplice. You're part of my legacy. If you've absorbed WoMBAT, laughed/thought/cried along the way, and caught the word-of-mouth bug, then guess what? Tag, you're it. The torch is in your hands now.

Welcome to the Family

By embracing these ideas, you've basically joined my not-so-secret society of creative troublemakers. Welcome to the family! We don't have membership cards (yet) or a secret handshake (unless you count high-fiving a stranger after a marketing stunt), but we do have a shared mission. You carry the torch I lit years ago, and every time you use these frameworks, you keep that flame alive.

Remember WoMBAT? The mindset of "What Might Be All The...". (I hope so since I have mentioned it in every chapter) That little question-shifting trick is now your secret weapon too. When you start reframing problems with "What might be all the ways...," you're thinking like me (scary, I know). You're opening up possibilities instead of shutting them down. And you're officially carrying on the legacy of looking beyond the obvious, of asking the crazy questions others don't think to ask.

If you've ever laughed out loud or furrowed your brow in deep thought while reading this book, congratulations, you've experienced the Laugh, Think, Cry filter in action. It's not just a cute slogan; it's a way of life. If an idea makes you laugh, think, or cry, it's got soul. It's real. Hold onto that, and promise me you'll use it as your creative compass. From this day forward, every time you make someone double over with laughter, blow their mind with insight, or touch their heart, you're not just doing your job, you're doing our job. You're part of the legacy now, keeping the spirit of bold creativity alive.

Be Bold or Be Forgotten

Let's get one thing crystal clear: boldness isn't optional. It's the price of admission for creating unforgettable work. Playing it safe might keep you comfortable, but comfortable gets zippo in the memory bank. In case it wasn't obvious by now, I believe in swinging for the fences (or sometimes, jumping over them with a rocket-powered motorcycle). I've seen plenty of "nice enough" ideas come and go, and trust me, no one remembers them.

Throughout my career, people have remarked that I "have some balls" (their words, not mine...but I do and they are beautiful!) for the stunts I've pulled. They're not wrong. Those crazy stunts taught me a simple truth: if you don't risk the spectacular, you settle for the mediocre. Sure, not every bold idea will work. Some will flop majestically. But I guarantee you, the stuff that does hit will be the stuff of legend. And legends aren't born from tiptoeing to the line; they're born from dancing past it in a flame-retardant suit, grinning all the way.

So promise me this: from now on, when you're faced with a choice between a safe bet and a gutsy one, give safe a polite nod and then go break the rules. Be respectfully rebellious. Take the shot that scares you. Pitch the idea that makes your voice shake a little. The world has enough people coloring inside the lines; we need more brave souls scribbling in the margins, drawing monsters and unicorns and whatever else the rest of the world is too timid to imagine. Boldness is the only way forward. It's boldness or bust.

Inspiration Is Everywhere (Seriously, Everywhere)

If there's one thing I hope you've learned, it's that inspiration doesn't live only in marketing textbooks or case study PDFs. Inspiration is everywhere, and I do mean everywhere. One of the worst things a creative person can do is put on blinders and only look in the same places everyone else is looking. You've got to be the person who finds marketing wisdom in a Netflix comedy special, or spots a brilliant campaign idea in the middle of a graffiti mural on a back alley wall.

Open your eyes and your mind to the world beyond the boardroom. Go to an art gallery, binge-watch cartoons, eavesdrop on conversations at the coffee shop (I won't tell). Read a novel once in a while, or better yet, a comic book. Some of the best ideas I've ever had came from totally "non-marketing" sources. I mean, who else would connect a Where's Waldo puzzle to a lesson on creative focus and notice hippo dentists lurking in the corner? (If you got that reference, you've definitely been paying attention.)

The point is, if you only look where everyone else is looking, you'll only find what they've already found.

Make it a habit to seek out the unusual and the unexpected. Train your brain to say, "What might I learn from this?" about everything. Watch people, soak in experiences, fill your head with diverse influences. Because when the well of inspiration runs dry, it's usually because you've been dipping the bucket in the same tired stream as everyone else. Go find a new stream! Creativity is an adventure sport; get out of your comfort zone and explore. Your next great marketing idea might just leap out at you from a late-night taco truck or a Shakespearean sonnet, or who knows, maybe the way your dog insists on playing with exactly the one toy he's not supposed to. Stay curious, and you'll never run out of raw material for remarkable ideas.

Make Them Laugh, Think & Cry

Let's talk about emotion. If there's no feeling in your work, you might as well pack up and go home. Emotion and originality win, hands down. Every. Single. Time. People won't always remember what you did, but they'll remember how you made them feel, that's not just a cliché, it's neuroscience and marketing 101 rolled into one. So if your campaign isn't eliciting some kind of real reaction, back to the drawing board it goes.

You've heard me say it before: I have a tongue-in-cheek answer when someone asks how I managed to build passionate fanbases for the brands I've worked on. I tell them, "I made love to the customers."

This is true but what I actually did was make them laugh, think, and cry. In other words, I made them feel something. That's the Laugh/Think/Cry framework we've been harping on. It's a filter, a test, a challenge to yourself: does this idea provoke an emotional response? If yes, proceed. If not, it's back to the lab.

Humor, intellect, and heart, if you can hit at least two of those notes, you've got a fighting chance at a winner. Hit all three and you've struck gold (plus, you might earn yourself a statue in the Marketing Hall of Fame, or at least a free beer from a grateful client). Think about the ads, stories, or experiences that stick in your mind even years later. I guarantee you they either cracked you up, taught you something profound, or moved you to tears (heck, maybe all of the above in a single 60-second Super Bowl spot).

That's not an accident. Original ideas make us feel, and we pass those feelings on. Boring ideas might be perfectly serviceable, but "perfectly serviceable" isn't going to get anyone to share it at brunch or tweet about it with heart emojis.

So don't shy away from emotion. Double down on it. Be funny (even if a bit irreverent, you have my blessing to occasionally get weird, or even always get weird). But also be thoughtful and heartfelt.

Best case, you'll make a genuine connection with your audience. Worst case, hey, at least you won't be putting them to sleep. In a world where attention is the most scarce commodity, making people feel something is your secret sauce for staying memorable. So go ahead, make 'em laugh, make 'em think, or make 'em cry. Just make 'em feel.

Make Them Talk (The Word of Mouth Magic)

All these wild ideas and emotional stories we've discussed have one ultimate goal: word of mouth. The Holy Grail. The big enchilada. Call it what you want, it's the secret sauce that money can't buy (at least, not genuinely). If people are talking about you or your work when you're not in the room, you've done something right. Word of Mouth is the endgame of all remarkable ideas. It's literally the reason we aim to be remarkable, because we want people to remark about us.

Think about it: every stunt, every risky move, every laugh/think/cry moment, it's all designed to get people to lean over to their friend or fire up their group chat and say, "Holy shit, have you seen this?!" That's when you know you've transcended marketing and entered the realm of cultural conversation. And trust me, that's where you want to be. You want your brand, your idea, your project to live rent-free in people's heads and on the tip of their tongues.

The beauty of Word of Mouth is that it's a gift that keeps on giving. One person tells two people, who each tell two more, and suddenly you've got a movement.

But you can't cheat your way into it. You have to earn it by being bold and original, as we've hammered home. Remember, remarkable literally means worth making a remark about. So ask yourself whenever you're working on something: "Is this worth talking about? Would I tell my friends about this?" If the answer is no, either make it better or go back to brainstorming with a hearty dose of WoMBAT thinking until you hit on something that passes the dinner-party test.

I built my entire career on Word of Mouth marketing (heck, I've even been called one of the best at it, for what that's worth). But my real pride comes from seeing others pick up that mantle. Knowing that you, dear reader, are going to take everything we've talked about, the frameworks, the fearless mindset, and use it to get people talking about your crazy ideas next? That's better than any award. It means the mission continues. It means the world's about to get a lot more interesting.

Thank You (Now Go Make History)

Before I send you off to conquer the world with your creativity, I need to say thank you. Truly. Writing this book has been a wild ride down memory lane and into the future, and knowing that you've come along for the ride means more than I can express in a single paragraph (but I'll try). Thank you for reading my ramblings, for laughing (and possibly groaning) at my jokes, for thinking critically about what I've shared, and for being open enough to maybe even tear up at a story or two. You, the readers, are the reason I do any of this.

I also want to thank everyone who's fueled my creative career for the last twenty, thirty or forty years, depending on when you are reading this. To the folks who read my blog posts and newsletters way back when and encouraged me to keep pushing boundaries, you were the first spark. To every conference organizer and event host who ever handed me a microphone (what were you thinking?), thank you for trusting me to entertain and inspire.

To my partners in crime, the collaborators, teammates, and brilliant minds I've worked with (including those brave enough to join me from the Mad Magazine and Simpsons crews), you've made this journey a thousand times more fun and a million times more effective. To all the clients and companies that rolled the dice on a Saul Colt original™ idea, thank you for having the courage to say "yes" when "no" would have been the safer play. And to anyone out there who has ever believed in a crazy, brave, breathtaking idea, whether it was mine or your own, thank you for keeping that faith. You are my people.

…and when I say my people i mean the ones who befriended me, loved me, some even made love to me but mostly just inspired me to be bold personally or profession-ally. (in no particular order and I am sure I will forget some people)….Jenny Gershon, Mitch Joel, David Berkowitz, Jay Bernbaum, Jeff Goldenberg, Michele Romanow, Matthew Page, Steven Page, The Drew Blood, Jason Greenspan, Jeremey Rakowsky, Andrew D'Souza, Gregg Tilston, Dave Delaney, Andy Nulman, Ryan Coleman, Natalie Gooding, Dara Frank, David Crow, Brett Petersel, Joseph Jaffe, Bob Knorpp, Pamela Slim, Dave Coleman, Ben Zlotnick, Michael Nuss, Heather Ritchie, Jessie Frampton, Krista Neher, Sunir Shah, Mike McDerment, Levi Cooperman, Kim Bernbaum, Scott Monty, Dave Kerpen, Hana Abaza, Lisa Gotlieb, Brian Garside, Jeremy Pepper, Bill Morrison, Tim Stack, Wayne White, Paul Reubens, Ian Bear, Randy Matheson, Jennifer Sullivan, Danny Fingeroth, Joel Kleinberg, Dave Cove, Aaron Draplin, Jon Lazar, Dixie Laite, Brett Kimmel, D.J. Coffman, Raymond Roker, Mike Lee, Elizabeth Pigg, Nan Palmaro,

Carrie Kerpen, Whitney Matheson, Joshua Hale Fialkov, Skye Topic, Clint Schaff, Meghan Peters, Jay Baer, Jason Silva, Casey Boshae, Ross Richie, Jim Mahfood, Brian Michael Bendis, Mike Nolan, B. Clay Moore, Mimi Pond, David Feldman, Jelly Helm, Jackie Martling, Desaree Weeres, Hugh Forrest, Jesse Thomas, Frank D'Andrea, Reggie Wildman, Joe Anthony, Steve Garfield, Chris Brogan, John Wall, Stephanie Fierman, Micki Krimmel, Sarah Wilbore, Kasey Bayne, John Flasnburg, Frank Black, Billy Yost, Allan Branch, Joe Caserto, Tina Roth Eisenberg, Dylan Boyd, Annie Luchsinger, Chris Fason, Ben Zifkin, Stacey Panousopoulos, Jason Rodriguez, Kody Chamberlain, Jonathan Sackett, Natalie Bruss, David Dougherty, Paul Thorogood, Nicola Harris, Josh Fisher, Rob Ulman, Amber Naslund, Amber Mac, Mitch Soloway, Virgina Miracle, Cami Koas, Rick Turoczy, Jon Wye, Mallory Blair, Greg Galant, Kenyatta Cheese, Jeremy Tanner, Tim Shapcott, Andy Lark, Russ Fujioka, Steve Hoechster, Jeff Cutler, Ian Vacin, Ben Lucier, Sheldon Levine, Amanda Rappak, Brant Bonin Bough, Darrell Cox, Penn Jillete, Bobcat Goldthwait, Rick Rezinas, Max Major, Jason Lewin, Kelvin Kang, my loving family who I try to eat every shabbat dinner with and most importantly my friend and lawyer Stephen Turk who I hope doesn't get any calls regarding this book.

THIS MIGHT BE the end of the book, but it's not the end of the story, not by a long shot. Now it's your turn to get out there and create the kind of work that future marketers (and maybe their AI writing buddies) will reference with awe. Take these frameworks and make them your own. Put your unique spin on them. Blow my mind with what you come up with, nothing would make me prouder.

In the immortal words of basically every action movie: This is not goodbye. It's a hand-off. I'm passing the baton, the torch, the flaming nunchucks of creativity, whatever you want to call it, to you. I've shown you mine (ideas, that is but I like dirty pictures too); now I can't wait to see yours. Go forth and be bold, be fearless, be unforgettable....*and hey, if you made it this far you should totally spend 30 seconds and write me a 5 star review on Amazon!*

Thank you for sharing your time with me and if you ever need help drop me an email at saul@theideaintegration.com I am always here for you.

bonus chapter: ideas & ideation in the age of ai (and why this book might just save your soul)

I AM NOT the biggest fan of AI. I mean I use it and it is helpful, how it can speed things up, how it can help take an idea from "ehhh" to "holy shit!" with just a nudge and a prompt. I do love my AI sidekick (I let him pick his own name and he chose, Ruckas). But at the same time, I'm scared. Like, actual "clutch your pearls and scream into a pillow" scared. Because what we're watching right now is the shrinking of an industry we've all bled for, the slow erosion of creative professions by an unblinking, algorithmic tsunami.

You may have noticed I purposely didn't focus this book on specific platforms, tools, or tech stacks. That was intentional. Frameworks like WoMBAT and Laugh/Think/Cry are designed to be timeless, applicable whether you're brainstorming on a napkin, in a Slack thread, or using the most bleeding-edge prompt engineer interface in existence. But to *not* talk about AI right now would be ignoring the 10-ton cyborg elephant in the brainstorming room. It's on everyone's mind, for good reason. And it deserves its own spotlight, because it's changing the rules of the game.

We've reached the point where AI can write a jingle, design a logo, generate a brand story, animate a ballerina pirouetting on the Eiffel Tower while promoting crotch cream, and do it all in under 60 seconds. The new tools don't just assist; they *replace*. And we need to talk about it. Not in a panic. Not in a LinkedIn humblebrag about "learning to prompt better." But seriously. With our eyes open.

Because the question isn't "Will AI replace creatives?" It's "What kind of creatives will still matter when it does?"

Why Process Matters More Than Ever

This book, and more specifically, the *process* in this book **WoMBAT and Laugh/Think/Cry** isn't just a way to come up with better ideas. It's a fucking survival kit. In a world where content can be made by anyone with an internet connection and 99 cents worth of Midjourney credits, the only people who survive are the ones who know how to:

1 Create ideas with purpose.

2 Edit ideas with heart.

3 Craft messages with soul.

AI can mimic. It can remix. It can regurgitate. But it still can't *give a damn*. That's your job. And the only way to consistently give a damn is to have a process that keeps your work honest, human, and memorable.

WoMBAT in the AI Era

Let's go deep: *What Might Be All The...* is now a way to dance with AI instead of being eaten by it. Here's how:

1. Use AI for Input, Not Output

AI is a brainstormer. A collaborator. A first-draft machine. Don't make it the final voice. Use it to feed your WoMBAT list, "What Might Be All The weirdest ways to sell sunscreen to vampires?" Let it throw spaghetti at the wall. Then *you* decide which strands are cooked. Let the machine puke ideas so you can polish and punch them up into something only *you* could've thought of.

2. Challenge the Algorithm

Most AI outputs are safe. Boring. Beige. Your job? Punch holes in the safety net. Use the WoMBAT framework to push further. Example: If AI suggests "sponsor a beach volleyball tournament" for a shoe brand, your WoMBAT lens should ask, "What might be all the ways to make that idea go viral in a nursing home?" Now we're somewhere interesting.

3. Build Lists the Bot Wouldn't Dare Touch

The best WoMBAT lists are the ones that feel like bad ideas at first, "illegal," "impossible," or "so dumb it just might work." AI doesn't do that well. It's trained to play it safe. But *you* know where the line is, and how to dance on it.

Laugh / Think / Cry in an Age of Synthetic Emotion

Here's the wild part: AI can now write scripts that hit emotional beats. It can fake sincerity. It can imitate joy. But it still can't feel it. That's where *you* come in.

The Laugh/Think/Cry framework ensures your ideas aren't just clever, they *matter*. They connect. They last longer than a scroll.

• **Laugh**: Use AI to suggest 100 jokes. Then write one that would actually make your weird uncle laugh.

• **Think**: Ask AI for facts. Then twist those facts into something that slaps the audience in the forehead.

• **Cry**: Let AI suggest sentimental lines. Then rewrite them with *actual* empathy, because you've loved, lost, and lived through more than a training dataset ever could.

What Happens When We Stop Valuing Human Ideas?

Let's not sugarcoat this: we are watching a slow-motion creativity genocide. Tools like Google Veo 3 are making fully rendered commercials on demand, no crew, no camera, no cast, no coffee. Just prompts. And let's be real: that's incredible *and* terrifying.

We're entering a simulation economy. The influencer isn't real. The testimonial is generated. The audience? Doesn't care, *yet*. But once everything is fake, authenticity becomes priceless. And you know what drives authenticity? Actual people. Real stories. Big ideas with fingerprints and coffee stains on them.

We are not just competing with other agencies anymore. We are competing with machines that never sleep and never second-guess. So what's left for us?

The answer: our *taste*. Our *judgment*. Our ability to tell a client, "Yeah, that's a great prompt. But it's a shit idea."

Be Discoverable by Machines, But Loved by Humans

Here's where it all comes full circle: In the AI era, the way to win isn't by being louder. It's by being *mentioned*. If AI doesn't talk about you, neither will your customers. That means:

- Get quoted.
- Get published.
- Get talked about.
- Get good.

GEO, Generative Engine Optimization, is now more important than SEO. You need to show up in the content machines *consume*. If you're not cited, you don't exist. So start feeding the machine, but do it with *your* voice. Not some AI-mimic BS. Write weird. Speak loud. Be undeniable.

Final Thought: Don't Be Replaced. Be Remembered.

This book doesn't promise immortality, but it does promise *relevance*. You made it to the very end, you've seen the frameworks. You've seen the process. You know how the sausage gets made, and you know it still needs a human butcher to season it right.

Use AI. Love AI. But never let it *be* you.

Because the world doesn't need more content. It needs more *you*.

Now go make something worth quoting.

PS: *If AI ever tries to write a book like this, I hope it includes a chapter called "Why Banana Ads Still Slap" and footnotes about coffee-fueled meltdowns over font choices. Until then, we're safe.*

appendix: saul colt's interactive creative marketing toolkit

LAUGH / Think / Cry Idea Filter Worksheet

Saul Colt's secret sauce is emotional impact – he literally says he made his customers "Laugh, Think and Cry". Use this worksheet to filter and score ideas by their emotional punch. Bold, shareable campaigns often score high in at least one category. For example, Saul's famous FreshBooks banana-stand stunt at a tech expo was rated highest on Laugh – it played on the Arrested Development joke about "money in the banana stand," which had people laughing and tweeting.

Idea: _____

LAUGH (1–5): __ /5

THINK (1–5): __ /5

CRY (1–5): __ /5

· · ·

NOTES   /   Twist   Potential:

_____

EXAMPLE: FRESHBOOKS "BANANA STAND" – Laugh = 5 (hilarious Arrested Dev gag); Think = 2 (clever pun "money in the stand"); Cry = 0.

WoMBAT Brainstorming Worksheet

We ask "better questions than everyone else" using the CIA-inspired WoMBAT method (stands for What Might Be All The…). Fill in these prompts to unleash wild, wide-thinking brainstorming. Don't stop at the first idea – WoMBAT forces you to explore every angle. In one example, Saul's team asked, "What might be all the ways to bring 1970s Harlem to life?" – which uncovered the forgotten Harlem numbers racket.

Campaign   /   Brief:

_____

WOMBAT PROMPT #1: "What might be all the ways to _____?"

IDEA   1:

_____

IDEA   2:

_____

IDEA   3:

_____

· · ·

WOMBAT PROMPT #2: "What might be all the forgotten details of _____?"

IDEA   1:
_____

IDEA   2:
_____

IDEA   3:
_____

BONUS   PROMPT: "What   might   be   all   the crazy/unexpected ways to _____?"

IDEA   1:
_____

IDEA   2:
_____

IDEA   3:
_____

TOP   PICK   /   Big   Idea:
_____

. . .

GUIDANCE: Think broadly and weirdly. In the Harlem TV show example, these prompts uncovered a story element – "the Harlem numbers racket" – that became the centerpiece of a stunt.

Word-of-Mouth (WOM) Campaign Planner & Talk-Worthiness Rubric

Word-of-mouth campaigns live on buzz. Plan your stunt so people will want to talk about it. Outline the hook and then score how "talk-worthy" your idea is on key criteria. High scores mean big viral potential.

Campaign   /   Idea:

_____

HOOK   /   Unique   Angle:

_____

KEY   MESSAGE   /   Audience:

_____

WOM   ELEMENTS   (SHARE   TRIGGERS):

_____

INFLUENCERS   &   Channels:

_____

ESTIMATED   BUDGET   /   Resources:

_____

TALK-WORTHINESS SCORES (1–5):

. . .

NOVELTY / Surprise: __ /5

EMOTIONAL IMPACT: __ /5

EASE OF SHARING: __ /5

RELEVANCE / Interest: __ /5

TOTAL (MAX 20): __ /20

PROJECTED WOM REACH (E.G. SHARES, mentions):

_____

NEXT   STEPS:

_____

TIP: Higher scores = more buzz. Saul's stunts always aim for a 5 on Novelty – they're the sort of thing people "have to tell a friend about". Score your idea honestly, then boost the low categories if you can.

Case Study: FreshBooks "Banana Stand" Stunt

Challenge: A small accounting startup needed to stand out at a finance conference.

. . .

WOMBAT BRAINSTORM: Asked, "What cultural reference can small-business owners bond over?" (Answer: Arrested Development's banana stand.)

BIG IDEA: Recreate the Bluth family banana stand on the floor and give away 2,000 branded bananas.

EXECUTION: Built a 9-foot wooden banana booth, handed out bananas printed with the FreshBooks logo and a URL. The absurdity drew crowds – attendees snapped photos, joked "There's money in the banana stand," and shared on social media.

RESULT: Huge buzz for minimal cost. FreshBooks earned far more attention and sign-ups than with a normal booth. The stunt made people laugh (Laugh=5) and talk about the brand.

KEY TAKEAWAY: Align pop-culture humor with your brand. A simple, funny hook + free branded giveaway = major word-of-mouth.

YOUR TURN – FreshBooks Case Template:
   Challenge:

_____

BRAINSTORM   **PROMPT:**

_____

. . .

INSPIRATION   FOUND:

_____

BIG   STUNT   IDEA:

_____

EXECUTION   PLAN:

_____

EXPECTED   OUTCOME:

_____

CASE STUDY: HARLEM "PLAY THE NUMBERS"
Activation (TV Show Promo)

Brief: Launch a new 1970s Harlem-themed TV show with a bang.

WOMBAT DIVE: The team lived the culture – watched blaxploitation films and asked, "What might be all the ways to bring Harlem to life? What forgotten details could surprise fans?"

BIG IDEA: Reintroduce Harlem's old numbers game in real life. Actors in 1970s attire ran sidewalk "lottery parlors." Winners didn't get cash, but tickets to era-specific experiences (e.g. secret club night or a "1977 NYC Blackout" party).

. . .

PLAN HIGHLIGHTS: Vintage street setup; actors as bookies; branded tickets; themed parties with show stars and music.

POTENTIAL IMPACT: Immersive, newsworthy, and deeply emotional. By tapping rich cultural history, the stunt would get people talking and feeling connected.

KEY TAKEAWAY: Deep research unlocks gold. By WoMBAT-questioning Harlem's history, they turned a hidden detail into a shareable experience. Offer exclusive rewards (like secret events) to make the story worth telling.

YOUR CAMPAIGN TEMPLATE – Brainstorm to Breakout:
　　Campaign Brief: _____

INSIGHTS / Mood: _____

WOMBAT Q: _____

TOP IDEA (HOOK): _____

EXECUTION PLAN: _____

EMOTIONAL SCORE (L/T/C): L __ / T __ / C __

. . .

TALK-WORTHINESS SCORE (/20): __

METRICS   TO   TRACK:
_____

CAMPAIGN POSTMORTEM WORKSHEET

After launch, don't just move on – analyze everything. Be brutally honest and write it down.

What Worked: (Successes, what surprised people)
_____

WHAT FLOPPED: (Misses, awkward moments)
_____

WOM REACH (EST.): ($\approx$ # of conversations, shares, mentions) _____

PRESS & Social Lift: (Media features, followers gained)
_____

LESSONS LEARNED: (What to repeat or avoid next time)
_____

PRO TIP: Even Saul Colt debriefs every stunt. Remember, "we've never been punished for standing out" – but you'll learn from flops, so document them and adjust quickly.

Brainstorm Prompts by Campaign Type

Use targeted prompts to spark ideas for each scenario:

Events:

"WHAT'S the most jaw-dropping thing we could do live on stage?"

"WHAT WILL ATTENDEES brag about on social media during the event?"

PRODUCT LAUNCHES:

"IF OUR PRODUCT were a movie or character, what wild scene would it star in?"

"HOW COULD the product reveal itself with a surprise or performance?"

PR STUNTS:

"WHAT OUTRAGEOUS SPECTACLE could be newsworthy in our industry?"

"HOW CAN we involve bystanders as part of the stunt?"

PARTNERSHIPS:

. . .

"WHAT UNEXPECTED BRAND collab would get people talking?"

"HOW CAN we mash up two different worlds in one stunt?"

(BONUS TIP: Always end prompts with "why" or "how" to dig deeper into the idea.)

Personal Brand Alignment Worksheet

Even the craziest idea must fit you. If your personal or company brand is known for something, make sure the stunt delivers on that promise.

My Brand Identity: _____ (e.g. bold jokester, serious innovator)

CORE VALUES: _____ (e.g. honesty, fun, social good)

SIGNATURE STYLE: _____ (e.g. edgy humor, heartfelt, technical genius)

DEALBREAKERS: _____

(topics/stunts I won't do)

DOES this idea feel like me? [ ] Yes [ ] No

HOW I'LL MAKE It Unique to Me:

_____

. . .

REMEMBER: If the idea doesn't sound authentic in your voice, it won't land. Tick that box Yes only if it truly fits your brand personality.

Stakeholder Pitch Checklist

Before you pitch to bosses or clients, check all boxes. This ensures your presentation is bulletproof – and fun!

Clear Big Idea: Simple, punchy tagline or one-sentence description.

EXPECTED OUTCOME: What we want (e.g. media mentions, sign-ups, etc.).

PROOF POINTS: Similar successes or data (case studies, pilot results).

EMOTIONAL HOOK: Explain why people will care or laugh.

VISUALS / Mockups: Sketches or storyboards of the stunt.

PLAN & Timing: Key steps and a rough timeline.

BUDGET & Resources: Rough cost and people needed.

RISK & Mitigation: Potential issues (legal, PR) and safeguards.

. . .

NEXT STEPS: What you need (approval, funds) and how you'll launch.

PITCH LIKE SAUL: Enter with confidence and a grin. You're selling a story, not just a slide deck. Tick all these boxes, then deliver it with conviction – and maybe a surprise prop or two.

praise for saul colt

In my way too many years in show business, I've met so many wildly creative people. Most fall into the recesses of my immature brain but others linger. Saul Colt seems to never leave. And that's a great thing.

The greatness really shines in The Only Creative Process That Matters. Only Saul could make a self-help book about marketing an enjoyable romp.

— Tim Stack - My Name Is Earl, Night Stand, Curb Your Enthusiasm

Saul is the kind of marketer I aspire to be, bold, innovative, and unafraid to push boundaries. His ideas don't just turn heads, they move people to take action. With *The Only Creative Process That Matters*, I finally have a blueprint to infuse that same courage and clarity into my own marketing strategy. Saul's process isn't just creative, it's catalytic.

— Pamela Slim, author, speaker and agency owner

He's a bit like a mad scientist. He's so "out-of-the-box" that if you aren't inspired by his ideas, you just don't belong anywhere near Marketing. His premise of "laugh, think, cry." is simple, so why aren't more people doing it?

— Mark Soloway